More Cake

by Bonny Hoeflein

Table of Contents

Dedication

For Karl, who has demonstrated the unconditional
love of God to me since the day we met.

"When I found him whom my soul loves, I
held him and would not let him go.."

Song of Solomon 3:4 (Amp)

Foreward for Bonny Hoeflein

THERE ARE SOME MOVIES THAT you watch (sometimes over and over again) because you love a particular actor or actress. You can see them in one role and then suddenly, when you see them in another role, you fall right into line and find yourself caught up once more in their new character because you believe in them.

That's how it is with Bonny Hoeflein. Whenever she speaks, no matter what the subject matter may be, I am carried along by her wonderful persona and her imaginative way with words. Now she is finally doing what she was made to do. Bonny has written a book. It's called *More Cake*, and it is a great read!

I've known Bonny for over 30 years and I know one thing, she is one of the most real, honest, vulnerable, and wisest persons I've ever known. Oh, yeah, she is also hilarious! From the mid-60's till the late 90's America had Erma Bombeck, a humorist who brought a new and joyous approach to everyday life.

As long as I've known Bonny, I've seen her in that same light.

She understands daily life, and like Erma Bombeck, she is someone who brings that same humorous understanding of reality…but with a twist. Bonny also helps the reader understand that the journeys and trials of life are more than just a story to bring a laugh. Her bedrock of wisdom and her understanding of the ways of God will help every one who picks up *More Cake* to be filled with hope and excitement for who they are and where God is taking them.

As you read *More Cake* you will see that life has not always been easy for Bonny. She has, like all of us, been through the ringer, and yet, she is able to marry all she's gone through with all she's learned and as a result, we, the readers are the beneficiaries.

Bonny is a wife to an amazing man and a mother to three beautiful children. She knows what it means to abound and she knows how to find Him when things get tough. She has been an encouragement to so many over the years and a friend to all who come in contact with her.

It's my real pleasure to write this foreward and to steer your eyes and thoughts toward reading this book. *More Cake* is exactly what it sounds like. It's a feast for the heart and an invitation to see yourself and your life in a new and wonderful way. There is hope because He is our hope. Thank you Bonny for helping us see that more readily and for sharing your life so beautifully so that we can see His goodness and His faithfulness.

It's really true…we all need *More Cake*!

Chris DuPré
Pastor, Songwriter, and Speaker
Author of *The Wild Love of God, and Unstuck*

Preface

H I, I'M BONNY. I THOUGHT it would be nice to introduce myself and tell you a little bit about me. After all, isn't that what we normally do when we meet people or make new friends? To me, meeting new people ranks right up there with connecting with old friends. Love both. (Nice to meet you, by the way.) The same goes for new places and old hangouts.

I'm a wife, and I'm a mother of two teenaged daughters and one adult son who is newly married to my beautiful daughter-in-law. Feeding a houseful of hungry people makes me really happy. I wouldn't want to choose between parties and solitude, however. I need both.

Laughter is therapeutic. God is always speaking, always.

I'm a foodist. I love to garden. I was born in a make-up store, pretty sure.

On vacation, I'm obsessed with visiting universities and

churches. A walk in the forest, though, or on a beach restores me better than any tonic.

Creative atmosphere is energizing. Beautiful food is healing. Gifted writing is transcendent. And inspired music is magic.

I believe in mentoring, coaching, nurturing- or whatever else you want to call loving God and people, and I want to show others how to do the same. God has cared for me. The Body of Christ also has nurtured me, so I'm hardwired to nurture others. You see, I'm passionate about spiritual mothering for everyone, even tough customers. In fact, I feel compelled to provide the spiritual parenting that was lavished on me. That's why I've brought these essays together and presented them to you in this book.

In the essays that follow, I endeavor to demystify spiritual life. I firmly believe God shows Himself to us in our everyday lives. He speaks through our life experiences and the experiences of those around us. He talks to us through His Word and during times of study, worship, and fellowship. As you will soon see, He loves to teach me in real-life and thought-life encounters with Him and others. And I bet that's what He has planned for you, too.

Starting from Scratch

T HIS BOOK IS FOR ANYONE who ever wished she had a mentor, for anyone who wished she had someone to show her the ropes or tell her the inside scoop about living and being transformed by the power of the Holy Spirit.

I personally am not from a family of Bible quiz champions, Sunday school superintendents, or VBS directors. My family and I were unconscious of the Kingdom of God. We were completely unaware that a loving God was waiting to invade our world, but He was. Though my mother often said, "You can't make a silk purse out of a sow's ear," meaning you can't change the basic nature of a person, we discovered the *real* truth. Jesus *can* change a person. Trust me. I'm living proof, and so is my mother, by the way.

Life's not simple or easy for that matter. I've struggled in seasons of my life with being frustrated or jealous of people who seemed to be exempt from the same challenges I faced. I spent too much time wishing I was someone else because I didn't have an ideal family, a Barbie-doll body, or a normal attention span. Along the way, I found out I wasn't the only one thinking I'd never become what God intended—that it was hopeless.

Each of us grapples with our identity and purpose. We get lied into thinking, *I'm not smart enough or pretty enough. If only I were more productive or organized, if only I came from a different family, then I could really be somebody.* We can feel like we've been issued a jigsaw puzzle that's missing some pieces because our lives don't generate the life pictures we see other women enjoying. Our expectations are our own worst enemy. They rob us of our joy.

It doesn't help our cause when the culture these days wants to tell us that we'd be happier being a different, more improved us with newer stuff, like cooler clothes or a nicer place to live. *All I need is a hipster farm table covered with handmade pottery to serve my "farm to table" food,* you may have thought after too much time on Pinterest. Or, if fashion is more your thing, you may have asked yourself, *Wait, I need high-waisted jeans with flared legs?* Truth be told, some of us already did that.

Just maybe you're someone who's thrown off by people who have exotic experiences that they've blasted all over Instagram, where they're bathed in golden light and surrounded by their beautiful families on pristine beaches. Then again, maybe you're annoyed when your peers are recognized for their amazing achievements in an alumni publication, and you can't even get your laundry done.

Food and hosting, fashion and clothing, travel and leisure, professional achievements, or whatever else you may be after, the tribal knowledge I've discovered and want to share is this: I've decided that all this stuff is the frosting of life. It's nice but not really the true substance of living joyfully. There's always something that can rob me of my peace—a cool thing or place that can make me wish I was someone or somewhere else. My problem isn't that

I need more frosting (though I'll take it if offered). My problem is that I need more cake.

What if the essentials of real happiness aren't in the frosting of life but in the cake—the substance underneath the possession, the culture, and the status?

More Cake is about finding out what's really able to bring you peace and satisfaction. It's not a temporary topping. It's the permanent purpose. Your cake is the core and substance of who you were made to be, not the perceptions other people have of you or how the culture and social media define you. Your cake is the truth that unravels the lies you were told about your purpose and your significance. *More Cake* is about how to have more of what's important so that you can enjoy both the beautiful and broken parts of any given day. And at the end of the day, *More Cake* is about sharing all of that with others.

Part 1:
Cake Apprentice

Rise to the Occasion

EVERY TIME I READ THE story of Old Testament Saul, I'm saddened when I read this verse, "Now the Spirit of the Lord departed from Saul" (1 Sam 15:14). That's such a drag! It's also a little scary. It makes me wonder, *How did he let the anointing of God leave his life?*

From the first time we meet him in Scripture, Saul spends his whole life comparing himself to other people. When he initially meets Samuel, he's looking for his donkeys, and Samuel greets him, saying, "And to whom is all the desire of Israel turned? Is it not you?" referring to Saul's being God's choice for king of Israel (1 Sam 9:20 NIV).

Basically, Saul responds, "Who? Me? You talkin' to me?" as he looks over both shoulders and points to his own chest. "Why do you want me? I am from the least tribe, I am the least in my family, and my clan is weakest" (see 1 Sam 9:21).

Initially, you might see his humility as virtuous, but the truth is, Saul never sees himself as being God's man, being God's choice. What's worse, he doesn't allow anything or anyone, even Samuel, to change his thinking. He is so performance-based that, at first, he feels inferior because of his family background and refuses to accept the endorsement of Samuel, God's prophet.

God empowers Saul anyway to do lots of cool exploits. God empowers him to prophesy. God anoints him in battle. Still, Saul hides when the people go to proclaim him king. He hides behind the luggage.

Briefly, Saul moves in the authority or anointing God provides for him. He routs all the enemies of Israel and is successful in battle.

However, we soon see that his improper understanding of his identity rears its head again. This time, instead of feeling unworthy to be used of God, Saul decides that his accomplishments entitle him to defy God's order concerning who makes the sacrifice (should have been Samuel the prophet), what gets destroyed in battle, and what gets taken as plunder. The Lord instructs Saul to wipe out the town and everything in it, yet Saul decides to listen to the people who say, "Keep the cattle. Such a shame to waste nice cattle." Even after Samuel tells him the kingdom will be taken from him because of his rebellion, which breaks Samuel's heart by the way, Saul says, "I have sinned, yet honor me now before the elders and my people, walk up with me so I look good when we worship God" (see 1 Sam 15:30). Saul cannot walk in godly confidence or godly obedience because he cares more about how people see him than what God says. Ouch.

But, Saul, it was never about your appearance or your performance. It was always a matter of God's choosing and empowering you. Your job was to listen and obey.

My mother has a funny saying. She says, "He wouldn't be a member of a club that would have him." She uses it to describe people who struggle with haughtiness and inferiority at the same time. They always frame themselves outside the group and looking in. Feeling either inferior or superior to friends, coworkers, and family is true for all of us sometimes. We base our contentment on whether we look better or have achieved more than other people—more education or less, more money or less, more kids or less. We can feel "less than" in any area, thinking things like:

- *She has a better voice than me.*
- *I wish I was pregnant like her.*
- *Her house is so clean, not like mine.*
- *She has a cool job.*

I frequently struggle with these or similar thoughts. In my own life, I'm beginning to understand that I'm qualified because I'm found in Christ. He's perfect. I'm not. I'm with Him. He equips me, calls me, empowers me, and makes provision for me. My job, by His grace, is to listen and obey.

Continually making excuses for why we're not qualified probably exasperates God. The truth is, we may not be qualified, but that doesn't mean God can't use us. It means we must lean on Him. It requires our trusting Him to enable us to rise to the occasion. We must find our identity in being found "in Christ" as it's explained in the New Testament, specifically in Galatians and Ephesians. Perhaps the best thing to do is to move our focus onto some foundational truth—namely, we have a place in God's family. We can't get voted out or fired. We can't age out or be behind in our dues. We are part of the Body of Christ because He chose us. That's the kind of news that will make any day a great day!

Finger in the Frosting

I HAVE TO BE HONEST. I have more to say about Old Testament Saul. I've always viewed him as childish, self-absorbed, and possibly a little bipolar. He's reluctant to accept his role as the king. He's impatient and impulsive in his making sacred sacrifices without waiting for Samuel to arrive to do them and in his saving the best animals against God's decree. In general, Saul has an inflated opinion about his own opinion. He thinks he's smarter than God. Doesn't this sound like adolescent behavior?

To me, the contrast between Saul and David has always been so stark. David was a man after God's heart while Saul was a loser, more or less.

Recently, I read the accounts again, and I saw something that I hadn't seen before. Upon closer inspection, I read that God Himself chose Saul and revealed this to Samuel before Saul knew it, just as He had done regarding David. I also realized from the Scripture that Saul and David were both good looking.

When Samuel anointed Saul with oil to be king, the Spirit rushed in and transformed him into a new man (1 Sam 10:6). Samuel goes on to say to Saul, "Now when these signs meet you, do what your hand finds to do, for God is with you" (1 Sam 10:7). God transformed Saul. He chose and equipped him. God filled him with power to govern the people and to do exploits in battle. The Spirit of the Lord was active in David's life, too, enabling him to win battles.

I guess you could say that, in some ways, Saul and David weren't very different. Both men sinned because of their impulsivity. Saul sinned regarding the sacrifices. David sinned by committing adultery with Bathsheba and having her husband killed in battle.

Their chief difference was manifested in how they responded to being confronted about their sin. David responded with godly sorrow and genuine repentance. Saul seemed as if he were upset that he got in trouble, like a child who cried because he got caught with his hand in the cookie jar. He was defensive and blamed others.

Here's what I learned: The actual events in a person's life seem less important to God than the condition of the individual's heart.

Saul was equipped with anointing. He was chosen, but his heart was not tender. Tenderheartedness toward God must be the key in staying on the God-ordained path. God brings correction to each of us. The trick is to stay vulnerable enough to His voice so that even His discipline is seen and received as His love.

Being prayerful and listening so that when we're impulsive, self-absorbed, irresponsible, or sneaky like those guys, we can receive God's correction as His redirecting us, cleansing us, teaching us to be more like Jesus. My GPS calls it *recalculating*. We can accept the kindness of God that leads to humble, genuine repentance. We can receive a gracious rebuke when we've been caught with our finger in the frosting.

An Interesting Mix

I F PETER WERE ATTENDING A public school today, he would probably be classified as having attention-deficit hyperactivity disorder (ADHD) and possibly obsessive-compulsive disorder (OCD). He was impulsive and intense. He was the first to recognize Jesus as being the Messiah, yet moments later Jesus scolded him for suggesting that He not go to the cross. Peter jumped out of the boat to walk on the water, only to sink moments later. He cut off the ear of the servant of the High Priest in the Garden of Gethsemane during Jesus' arrest. Yeah, Peter was a real piece o' work. After defending Jesus in the Garden, he followed Him to the court of the High Priest only to deny that he ever knew Jesus. This, he did, not once, but three times! (This guy makes me look stable.)

Peter was a real mixture.

After the resurrection, Jesus made special overtures to repair His relationship with Peter and then commission him to feed His sheep. Peter went on to be impacted by the Holy Spirit on the

Day of Pentecost and, subsequently, turned the world upside down for good.

In the end, the impulsive guy with little formal education—the one who was somewhat insightful but also presumptuous—was a key person in the establishing of the Kingdom of God in the first century church. Not bad.

I can relate to being a little impulsive myself, sometimes biting off more than I can chew. I've assessed situations too quickly and made the wrong call or haven't accurately counted the cost for my big idea, the cost being higher and the road longer than I ever dreamed. The story of Peter is comforting to me. He has higher highs and lower lows than most people. That wasn't new news to Jesus. He has strived with the tough customers, the impulsive, the compulsive, the hyperactive, and the wing-nuts.

Peter's life encourages me because sometimes it's difficult for me to remember that everyone experiences highs and lows. All too often, I feel like I'm the only one. Although people's posts on Facebook and Instagram look like they have perfect lives where everyone is always laughing in golden sunlight with guitars, at some point their lives they have sorrow, too. I know they do. Some of us seem to experience more extreme ups and downs, but maybe that's because we love the adrenaline, or maybe we just feel things deeply. Perhaps we simply forget the great moments too quickly. I am comforted by looking at the life of Peter because eventually he learns the true source of his identity, the source of his peace and his joy.

The story of Peter is how the transforming grace of God and the real power of the Holy Spirit were showcased in his life. God didn't just make him brave, but by the time he wrote the New Testament letters called First and Second Peter, Peter was talking about how to love one another earnestly from the heart. He said,

But you are a chosen race, a royal priesthood, a holy nation, a people for his own possession, that you may proclaim the excellencies of him who called you out of darkness into his marvelous light. Once you were not a people, but now you are God's people; once you had not received mercy, but now you have received mercy. (1 Peter 2:9-10)

And then said, in 1 Peter 4:10, "Serve one another as stewards of God's grace."

Peter's completely transformed thinking is rather miraculous! So what if it took him a whole lifetime? God radically changed his understanding about his identity, transformed him. In my book, that's still amazing.

Your Own Mix

Y OU'VE PROBABLY HEARD THE ILLUSTRATION that demonstrates how life is like a mayonnaise jar with the most important things in your life being represented by big rocks you place in the jar. You can only fit a few big rocks in your jar, and they should go in first so they will fit. The rest of the jar you fill with smaller rocks and sand—less important activities like grocery shopping and mowing the lawn—you know, the stuff we'll get to sooner or later.

In any event, each of us is allotted the same number of hours in a day, and no matter how many books are written on success, ultimately, the result is between us and God. Decisions about how you spend your time, money, and energy should be arrived at prayerfully or else those precious commodities are wasted.

I know people whose big rocks in their jar involve sport tryouts, practice transportation, equipment, and game schedules. Other families are highly committed to their music, lessons, auditions, costumes, rehearsals, recitals, and the show! The lives of many of the families I know revolve around the local church, worship practice, youth group, and outreaches. Maybe you're committed to Boy or Girl Scouting. It's amazing how parents reproduce their priorities in their kids.

Each of us should ascertain what God is saying and what He is blessing. Maybe it isn't about being balanced but rather managing the stewardship of our gifts and callings.

Here's the trick: People reflect God's image in different ways, not unlike the facets of a gem. I think we need to prayerfully trust God for the mix He has custom-designed for each of us. Then, we need to confidently follow those God-breathed paths while giving those around us permission to be different. This way we can cultivate greatness in our households. We can identify what God has gifted us in from birth and faithfully grow it. We can celebrate diversity of vision or burden. Unapologetically. We can stop being threatened by people who are doing their mix differently than we are and accept that that's always been God's plan. Sameness and conformity are not synonymous with holiness and goodness.

God doesn't want to homogenize us. He designed us to be different from one another. Your mix can be different from my mix. How freeing is that?!

Recipe Variations

THE CHURCHES AND COLLEGES I had attended in my teens and twenties tended to be focused on personal salvation, private holiness, preserving God's presence in us, hearing prophetically, moving in the miraculous, and winning souls. The church messages concentrated on how I could improve my personal experience with God and help others find similarly satisfying intimacies in prayer, Bible reading, and fellowship. For parishioners in this environment, understanding how they could implement Kingdom principles on earth was electrifying.

More recently, I have been made aware of a different stream, or community of Christian faith, whose distinctive message has more to do with advocating for the marginalized, stewarding the planet we live on, fighting poverty and hunger, and being more generally energized by activism. These brothers and sisters are not negating the reality of heaven; they are acknowledging that it is the call of the church to usher in the Kingdom of heaven in our current reality. These folks champion the helping vocations such as social work, education, medicine, law enforcement, and even environmental science as being avenues to bring godly solutions to this earth.

The problem comes when decisions should be made concerning finite resources like time, money, energy, and talent, and how they get spent. People's passions get hot, and it can be difficult to walk in agreement in these matters.

The only answer I can come up with is this: Unless we as brothers and sisters in Christ can be prayerful, we won't be able to be secure enough in our own callings to validate the possibility that God wants both agendas to succeed. Maybe being focused on just heaven or just earth is not God's ideal, but rather promoting both simultaneously.

If I perform the personal actions that God has called me to do, it doesn't negate that you may equally be called to a different burden, passion, or calling. We can witness by using our lives to bring redemption to this earth while also continuing to grow in our understanding of the King and the Kingdom of heaven as equally important in advancing God's agenda. Maybe we can make safe places to learn from one another and humbly teach one another while acknowledging our individual callings. If one of these sides of the redemption coin seems more important to you, it may be that you are a specialist in that area, and that was God's intention the whole time!

Prize Winners

D ID YOU EVER WAIT IN the dentist's office and all there was to do was read the framed diplomas and plaques on the wall declaring how much schooling the practitioner had accomplished? We've all seen the diplomas for advanced training in dentistry and certificates of dental coursework, seminars, workshops, and intensives for professional development.

Myriads of plaques and certificates are on the wall to convince me that the dental team is highly qualified to take electric power tools to my teeth, to inject drugs in my gums, and to permanently install a variety of metals, porcelains, resins, and plastics into my mouth. The wall art is supposed to inspire me to trust them. I get it.

As I was talking to a friend yesterday about the stuff she had endured throughout her childhood—parents destroyed by substance abuse, unstable home life, premature death, feelings of anxiety or abandonment—I could relate. I could have added adulthood hurdles that included infertility, miscarriage, adoption, and the roller coaster of raising a baby on the autism spectrum. It was as if we were comparing rodeo scars or tattoos. There wasn't really the same intense pain associated with my memories as there once was. Thank God, He had visited me in those areas of woundedness. He had taken away the pain and left a deposit of Himself, kind of like fillings in my teeth.

In areas of my heart that were painful, God has replaced my sorrow with testimonies that are not unlike the trophies and plaques on the wall of my dentist's office. I went through stuff, endured the process, believed for healing, learned to apologize and forgive, and came out knowing what I had not previously known about the faithfulness and mercy of God. Those testimonies are meant to be markers to point to when I go through yucky, painful seasons or when I discover that there are still areas of my life that need to be yielded or renovated—those areas that have not yet been transformed by the love and power of the Holy Spirit. The memories of when I discovered God's faithfulness are intended to make me brave.

Scripture says that, ultimately, we will see Jesus seated on the throne in heaven (Heb 12:2); furthermore, "the twenty-four elders" will throw their crowns at His feet (Rev 4:10). I always wondered what the crowns were and where they came from. Perhaps they are like trophies or prizes. They are accolades that were hard won. What I lay at the feet of Jesus are the moments in my life when I chose to trust Him, chose to lay down my rights and my own understanding. And in doing so, I was able to stand back and see the salvation of God.

Heavenly Filling

SOMETIMES, WHEN I READ THE Proverbs, they feel like braces on my teeth. They are necessary for correcting unhealthy, crooked places in my thinking and my actions.

The comparison between where I am and where I want to be can be painful at times. I just read, "A soft answer turns away wrath" (Prov 15:1 NKJV). I ought to put that on my wall somewhere.

Fortunately, if the Proverbs pinch my carnal places, the Psalms validate the fact that at least I'm not alone in my emotional ranting and raving. The Psalms surround me with reminders of how much God loves me and how I can worship Him for who He is regardless of my situation. The Psalms help my mind and emotions connect with God's heart and His presence. The Psalms also show me that I can be honest with God even when I'm frustrated. David occasionally asked God to break the teeth of his enemies! That's a pretty graphic image, and anything having to do with teeth makes me wince. It's nice to know that I'm not the only one with flare-ups.

The Holy Spirit is committed to helping us conform to the image of Christ. It's an ongoing process, and frankly, it's getting easier in some ways. I fight His leading less and repent faster than I used to. On the other hand, the thing that's harder is that I keep expecting to outgrow childish responses like feeling threatened by and jealous of other people. I went to a seminar last week on the effects of childhood wounds and abuse on our souls. I've heard it before; wounds and abuse from early childhood affect how we think and act later in life because they affect the way we view God. I think those issues are like cavities in our souls that the Holy Spirit wants to drill the pain and sin out so that He can fill us with Himself, enabling us to become stronger, more useful, and less vulnerable to seemingly random emotional pain. When He visits those places, cleans out the lies, and fills them with the truth of His love and goodness, we are more able to enjoy Him and His people.

I went to the dentist recently. Can you tell?

Cake: Comfort Food

IF YOUR KID HAS EVER owned Velcro sneakers, you know that over time the Velcro fills up with fuzz, lint, and dirt, keeping the two sides from sticking to each other. The two sides lose their ability to adhere. It's time for new sneakers.

Sometimes, I meet people, and it seems like the Velcro of their hearts no longer has the ability to stick or attach to new people. The little fasteners of their hearts are full of lint, inhibiting the little hooks of affection.

You know what I think? I think that getting older is inevitable, but becoming wiser is not. If we're not careful, the vulnerable places of our hearts become desensitized, which is the result of emotional fatigue and relational injury. If we're not careful, we become introspective and self-protecting. We no longer want to meet new people, make more friends, or reach out to others.

Why do we end up with lint on the Velcro of our hearts? Why

is it that our ability to make meaningful connection seems to have lost its shelf life?

Perhaps we have been betrayed by people we love. They let us down in either big or small ways. Our trust is injured because the ones we love have hurt us. Maybe we have simply grown weary in staying connected or reaching out. Psalm 55:12-14 says,

> It is not an enemy who taunts me—I could bear that. It is not my foes who so arrogantly insult me—I could have hidden from them. Instead, it is you—my equal, my companion and close friend. What good fellowship we once enjoyed as we walked together to the house of God (NLT).

It's hard to trust again after having been betrayed or disillusioned. Then, there may be times when the sorrow of good friends moving away or passing away makes us withdraw our hearts. Sometimes the seasons of life change, and we lose contact. It gets fatiguing. The desire to extend ourselves on behalf of someone else can lose its appeal. Being connected may seem like more trouble than it's worth. You just get tired.

I know someone whose faith got injured when she went through a tough season. She felt like, "God, if this is how You care for Your beloved child, You and me got issues." Sometimes, when you come out of the wilderness, God Himself must comfort you and allow you to heal. Faith needs to be restored, like the girl in Song of Solomon who comes up out of the desert, "leaning on her Beloved" (8:5 NIV).

In the end, I believe that our best life is one of continually being refreshed so that we can water others with the love we have received. It's valuable to take inventory every now and then to see if there is lint that's keeping the Velcro of our hearts from being attached to people. I believe that God Himself can remove the lint. We are renewed by allowing Him to refresh us, to come in and clean out the fuzz. When we allow God to heal us, we are free to be on the adventure of loving others—people who God has planned for us to love all along.

Lord, I thank You that I have the capacity to water and refresh other people. I pray that not only would I become a better lover and servant of other people, but that I would also teach my children how to love and serve. Help us to grow our capacity to see the needs of others and to be moved to be the answer to those needs. Don't let my children grow up oblivious to the needs of the world, and show me where to sow with my time and energy. Amen.

Is It Fresh?

SOMETIMES, WHEN I HAVE A container full of leftovers in my refrigerator, if they get super old and smelly, I'm afraid to open the container. I make my husband do it. If rancid dairy products smell bad, and rotten potatoes really stink, then I'm here to tell you that forgotten mashed potatoes contain the mix of both and are the worst! The container was bulging, and the contents looked green, pink, and furry, like the product of a diabolical chemical weapons lab. Mass destruction by stench. In the end, we threw out the whole container unopened. It wasn't worth the risk.

In John 11, we read about Mary and Martha's call for Jesus to come while Lazarus is getting sicker. The girls are hurt and a little confused when Jesus doesn't come until after Lazarus is dead. "Lord, if you had been here, my brother would not have died" (v. 32 NIV). Translation: "Where on earth have You been?!"

Ironically, Mary, who had sat at Jesus' feet, has the same

identical answer as her sister Martha. All that sitting didn't make her much more insightful than her sister.

So, when Jesus finally does arrive and He instructs them to take away the stone, Martha, ever the practical one, says, "Lord, by this time there is a bad odor, for he has been there four days" (John 11:39 NIV). As if Jesus doesn't know this detail?

Sometimes, the Lord instructs us to bring up an issue to which our first inclination is, "Lord, I've dealt with that. I don't want to revisit that. It smells bad, and frankly, it might be embarrassing and unpleasant. I don't have the bravery or strength to revisit the heartbreak, disappointment, or injury."

God is asking us to let Him come visit these areas that make us perpetually sad and tired—places of disappointment, confusion, and loss. He wants us to roll away the stone.

God wants to bring power, deliverance, perspective, and healing to us, and He desires those around us to help us out of our grave clothes. "Unbind him, and let him go," Jesus said (John 11:44). The Bethany girls never saw that coming!

When I am in the middle my painful moments and seasons, I need to remember that I don't always see the whole picture. The timetable of when God chooses to resolve my "issues" is not always in my control. Like Martha, I'm tempted to say, "Um, let's not go there. It's gonna stink."

It's possible that when God finally comes to shed light on these problem areas for me and the people I love, it will be the time when enough grace, love, support, and understanding are available for my healing. It will be the perfect time.

Pearlized Layers

D ID YOU EVER CONSIDER THAT woundedness and evil go hand in hand? You may have heard these expressions: "Crushed people crush people," "Shamed people shame people," or "Victimized people victimize people." We could go on and on about how bad spiritual legacies are perpetuated.

Not much has changed since biblical times, especially human nature. It's essentially the same. People tend to reproduce what they've learned. So how do I pray for the wicked? Do I pray for their destruction? An occasion to be hurt or offended is as pervasive now as it ever was. Is there any hope?

As you can tell, I've been thinking. How about this: Perhaps the point of woundedness in a person's life is like the invasion of a grain of sand into an otherwise happy oyster. The oyster covers its source of "pain" with layers of something smooth and beautiful called *nacre*. The nacre is deposited until finally a lustrous pearl is formed.

Like the Healing Balm of Gilead, the grace of God can cover places of injury the way the oyster covers the irritation of the grain of sand. Like nacre, the grace of God is poured out to cover our wounded places. The Spirit of God wants to come and heal the hurting places, lance festering memories, drain lies, and remove guilt and shame. The blood of Jesus has the power to cleanse. The mercy of God brings the power to forgive.

Potentially, what issues forth is the beautiful luster of a new lineage of redemption. The *agape* love of God has the supernatural ability to soothe and smooth, correct and instruct, not by rewriting history, but by redeeming it one labor-intensive pearl at a time.

Each encounter with a painful memory is another chance to put a layer of the pearl nacre of the luminous presence of God into that wounded place. Little by little, layer by layer, a breathtakingly, beautiful testimony of redemption is built; a treasure that no one can ever steal or destroy is cultivated. Jesus, the living God, who is the Pearl of Great Price, makes Himself known and felt and seen in the middle of your brokenness. He takes it and makes you altogether new.

Taste and See

PSALM 34:8 SAYS, "OPEN YOUR mouth and taste, open your eyes and see—how good God is. Blessed are you who run to him" (MSG). The psalmist encourages us to experience God's nature for ourselves. Doing so can bring fresh vigor to our lives.

God's very nature is good. It's redemptive. He is more interested in fulfilling His dream for your life than you could possibly imagine. He's not preoccupied with what's fair. We probably don't deserve as many chances as God wants to give us. He's generous that way. He continually ushers us into fresh opportunities to get it right. His desire is to restore us.

Matthew was originally called Levi. He was a tax collector who swindled people. He was greedy and self-indulgent, but Jesus called him to follow Him. The Twelve weren't necessarily in the Talented Tenth in their local schools, not top scholars in Hebrew School, but God chose them. They weren't chosen because they were compassionate and wise. They were self-seeking and cowardly when they first encountered Jesus. He chose them because He delights to showcase His redeeming love.

God has lessons that He wants to teach us so that we are transformed on the inside. He continually works with us to make us more like Jesus. It doesn't matter how good looking we are, what our family background is like, or how much education we have. God wants to showcase His glory through us. We're just the clay lamps that contain the brightness of His glory.

God wants to bring redemption through us to not only our lives, but to those of others around us. We can be change agents in the places where we find ourselves living, working, playing, and just doing regular life. You have the potential to allow the Holy Spirit to let His grace abound through you while you play on teams, serve on committees, at the places where you shop and where your kids go to school. You can be the person who thinks and acts redemptively. Your life can make people hungrier for God, or it can be like a bad smell that ruins people's appetite for Him.

In some realms of life, we're told it's too late to master something once we're grown. God doesn't think that way, however. Moses was eighty when God used him mightily. Noah, Caleb, Abraham, and Sarah did not win any prizes early in life like teenage, contest-winning popstars. The Bible says that they were advanced in years. They could have carried AARP cards. God doesn't work on our timetable.

God doesn't disqualify people, either. Sometimes, they disqualify themselves through pride, shame, or unbelief, but He delights to take "the foolish things to confound the wise" (1 Cor 1:27 KJV).

God's hallmark is that He delights to redeem lives, relationships, and any situation that may seem impossible to us. He doesn't always respond the way we want Him to or in a way we understand. He wants us to trust Him to be acting on our behalf and on the behalf of those people in our respective paths. God is a redemptive God!

God is a source of nurture. He is your best Momma and Daddy! Good parents provide, protect, instruct, direct, correct, and inspire. I can tell you that God Himself is the best example of a great parent and indeed is the best source of those nurture-based commodities. The Lord is not only the author of spiritual and natural parenting, but He also can compensate for any lack or neglect you've suffered no matter how severe. God can take the worst wounds of your soul and place on them the healing balm of His Holy Spirit.

Old Testament Joseph started out in a loving home, but at a young age he became the victim of a plot that originated in his father's house. He was betrayed, beaten, sold, mistreated, slandered, imprisoned, and forgotten. Yet God could use his life not only to save his family, but the future nation of Israel, and that was only the beginning.

Joseph's testimony of faithfulness in the face of adversity has inspired people of faith from that day until this present time. He is a beautiful type of Christ.

God had to protect Joseph. God Himself instructed and directed him. The Lord inspired him to not lose heart and ultimately gave him the interpretation of Pharaoh's dreams.

In the New Testament, the Lord Jesus is patient with His disciples. He instructs them, corrects them, and defends them. How like a mother He is when He tells the disciples to come aside, rest, and eat. Then, we see Him teaching them as He feeds the five thousand. Later, He defends them from the criticism of the Pharisees.

The Lord can nurture our dreams. He believes in us, delights in our valiant attempts, and sympathizes with our weaknesses. He is cheering for us as much as any parent standing on the sidelines at a sports event is supporting his or her child. He is able to resource our dreams and desires better than any human parent. Think about it.

And when we have outgrown our places in the homes we grew up in, whether it was a great Christian family, a warped place with painful memories, or someplace in-between, God desires to continue to form us for Himself. Long after we've stopped getting taller, it is His desire to teach us about his nature and heal our wounded souls. He is committed to growing us into mature daughters who are equipped to partner with Him to do cool things in the earth. He doesn't want self-absorbed daughters who are oblivious to the needs around them.

O, taste and see! God is good!

Part 2:
Cake Fundamentals

Florets

WHAT IF YOUR LIFE IS like a garden? Hopefully, there will be some nice things already there, even when the garden is new—stuff like brains and beauty. Perhaps there will be attributes like a lovely voice or athletic talent, maybe some type of intense drive or musical ability.

As a child, the garden of your life gets tended by other people. Like a new garden, you are little and at other people's mercy as to what gets cared for and planted. Hopefully, careful and caring people will lovingly feed and water the good gifts and seedlings. They will study the wind, weather, and sun exposure; they will provide support, feed your talents, steward and guard your gifts. They will pull out the weeds—things like unbelief, pride, self-centeredness, and laziness. They will bring other mentors and teachers into your life, who will also coax the best fruit and flowers into being. They will painstakingly kneel and plant faith, humility, peace, and patience. All things being well, they will water everything with prayer.

It's also possible that what was planted when the garden was new was not cared for or tended at all. Then, as an adult, the difficult work of weeding needs to happen. Emotional injuries, wrong thinking, bad perceptions, and misconceptions can be painful to remove. Dangerous habits and relationships are hard to dig up.

At some point, the stewardship of the garden gets transferred to the owner of the garden, you. You become responsible for your time, money, gifting, and affection, in addition to who comes into your garden and who's allowed to stay. You will need to weed out offenses, temptation, and bitterness. You will have to make sure the planting of passionate faith is not allowed to get too cold or dry.

Through it all, the Master Gardener is faithful to coach you and instruct you. He has a beautiful vision for you as a fragrant, fruitful garden. He has the tools and the knowledge. He knows what to uproot and tear out. He also knows how to plant, water, and tend. Isn't it fabulous news to know that He's committed to seeing His beautiful plan for your life brought to completion? He never gives up.

Don't Open That Oven!

WHEN A GIRL IS EIGHTEEN years old, she's usually fully grown. In this culture, she officially has the liberty to move away from her mother's house and, perhaps, live in a dorm. She is ready for adulthood to happen. She is ready for some type of impartation in the form of education, direction, and new experiences. She begins to meet those who will affirm and sharpen her gifts. They will give her a vision of what an impact her life can have or how she can make a difference in the world. It's time for people who will generally point out how much potential she has.

This is also a time in a girl's life when she radiates the beauty and freshness of her youth. She is attracting male attention. It should be a wonderful time, and it reminds me of when fruit trees bud in the spring. They are covered with beautiful blossoms which are often pink or white. They are fragrant, and people just like to be around them.

The next season of life can be trickier. Hopefully, you go into adulthood with a whole pocketful of dreams. You have ideas about what your husband will be like, what your children will look like, and what your ministry aspirations and vocational goals are. You should be chock full with a whole bunch of expectation. These expectations can be put on you by your family, friends, church, or culture. Frankly, our expectations might originate in our own minds.

The way I see it is, all those pretty blossoms got pollenated, and petals fell off. What you now have on your hands is more than just potential; you have promise. The flowers turn into little green fruit in the form of new marriages, pretty babies that need to be lovingly attended to, starter houses that need care and creativity, and beginning careers which require energy and brain power. It's easy during this season to feel like the dreams that you had about changing the world were just a lot of smoke. Everything requires attention, and nothing is finished. It can be exhausting. Some of the fascinating activities you used to do, don't happen anymore, at least not three times a week!

This is an extremely important season because, if you get confused, you might accidentally jeopardize all the emerging fruit. Your spouse is no longer tan and buff. Children require tons of time and money. It can be a season of obscurity, especially for women. Careers may require more concerted effort than you envisioned or may have to be finessed or adjusted. Using your gifts and talents may or may not happen every single day, unless you find the washing machine more fascinating than I do.

If, however, we can confidently continue to water these matters with faith and godly confidence, and if we can hear voices that spur us on to love and faithfulness, in due season this same life will be laden down with mature fruit that comes from perseverance. Your life will help sustain others by virtue of the fact that you have a testimony of God's faithfulness, which no one can negate. The dreams may be fulfilled in strange ways and in weird sequences. That's okay. The season for the big creative dream might come later. Tommy Lee Jones, Morgan Freeman, Helen Mirren, and Jamie Lee Curtis only became household names in acting after they turned fifty.

You must have the guts and determination to continue to water and tend until God brings what He promised, and you should support your friends to do the same. Don't be discouraged in the process. Sometimes, when a cake is at that crucial stage of rising, you shouldn't open the oven door because the cake will "fall" or fail to rise. Even though you're tempted, don't open that door. Let the cake bake!

The Missing Ingredient

I WAS A VARSITY DAYDREAMER. I don't know about boys, but when little girls are faced with ongoing, unpleasant situations, we fantasize that the whole scenario is different. We secretly pretend we belong to happy, well-adjusted families where the father is protective, wise, and funny. Our insightful, stylish, well-connected mother makes cool things happen, and our siblings are loyal and generous. The parents are perfect mentors, and laughter and music are on the menu every day. The faces of these fantasy family members are usually either TV characters or teachers and are subject to change. If any of this sounds familiar to you, you're in good company.

In the novel, *The Secret Life of Bees,* the central character is a little girl whose mother has died, and she seems determined to find the maternal love she lacks. I think that can be true of many of us who have an unquenchable thirst for an affectionate patron, a perfect parent. In the end, she receives the love she needs from a household full of women who, ironically, knew her mother.

I was reading Ezekiel 16. It depicts the allegorical picture of how God dealt with the people of Israel as with a beautiful girl. This is an excerpt of what God said in that chapter:

> On the day you were born, no one cared about you. Your umbilical cord was not cut, and you were never washed, rubbed with salt, and wrapped in cloth. No one had the slightest interest in you; no one pitied you or cared for you. On the day you were born, you were unwanted, dumped in a field and left to die. But I came by and saw you there, helplessly kicking about in your own blood. As you lay there, I said, "Live!" And I helped you to thrive like a plant in the field. You grew up and became a beautiful jewel.... I made a covenant with you ... and you became mine. Then I bathed you and washed off your blood, and I rubbed fragrant oils into your skin. I gave you expensive clothing of fine linen and silk, beautifully embroidered, and sandals made of fine goatskin leather. I gave you lovely jewelry, bracelets, beautiful necklaces, a ring for your nose, earrings for your ears, and a lovely crown for your head. And so you were adorned with gold and silver. Your clothes were made of fine linen and were beautifully embroidered. You ate the finest foods—choice flour, honey, and olive oil—and became more beautiful than ever. You looked like a queen, and so you were! Your fame soon spread throughout the world because of your beauty. (vv. 4-14 NLT)

The story goes on to say that even after all that attention and affection, the beautiful bride, Israel, was unfaithful, but that's not my point. I was amazed as I realized that God Himself is able to provide for my needs. He understands my hunger. Like the girl in the passage in Ezekiel, God sees me and makes provision *for me!* The passage says that, when the Lord first sees this little girl, she is abandoned and filthy. He, the Lord, sees her, makes provision for her, cares for her, and loves her!

I don't have to be like the girl in the allegory, ungrateful and rebellious. I can respond with thankfulness and humility. Instead of reacting like an orphan, I can accept being included, adopted, and loved. I can respond in gratitude and in anticipation for whatever else the Lord has planned.

I know it's weird, but even though I know that Jesus loved me enough to die for me, demonstrated His power by rising from the dead and sending the Holy Spirit to instruct and comfort me, this passage illustrates His ability to cleanse, transform, and celebrate me as a daughter and a woman. That, to me, is breathtaking.

So, in the matter of nurture, what you're supposed to receive from a loving mother and father—in matters of provision, direction, instruction, and wisdom—I believe that whatever is missing from your childhood story can be made up for by a loving God who continually delights to demonstrate His power on your behalf and mine.

From my earliest memories, God has brought faithful people into my life to provide what was missing. When there wasn't anyone to fill that void, God Himself came to me in the form of comfort from His Word or provision which took the form of favorable circumstances. It might have looked like good luck to some people, but I know all those coincidences were orchestrated by the hand of God.

All Decked Out

I CONFESS THAT, ALTHOUGH I DON'T subscribe to those glossy, expensive, fashion magazines, when someone I work with leaves them in the faculty room, I can't resist them. I'm dying to know whether ponchos are coming back for real people (they are), what hemlines are in style, and how wide pant legs should be.

My sister wore bohemian styles back in the seventies, and those have been back in style for quite a while, as have disco-inspired platform shoes and floppy hats. High boots? Low boots? Both! Will hosiery ever be popular again? These little details are so exciting to me.

Make-up trends are also electrifying. For example, I'm seeing either bold red or nude lips and not much in between. When I was attending Bible college my mother said to me, "Every time you come home from that school, you're wearing more make-up. You look like you fell in it!" It was true.

Looking again at Ezekiel 16, I so appreciate that God talks

about providing for the one He loves in the language of fashion, cosmetics, perfume, and jewelry. He doesn't condemn all those gorgeous details; instead, God provides and understands them. After all, He created them. I love that He gets my desire for artistic expression in the form of fashion! It's awesome to know that God speaks my language.

So, go ahead. Express yourself. God isn't asking you to be one person in church and a different person at the mall. He wants you to know that He loves your individuality. He made you with preferences and an eye for the details that please you.

Whether you're a floral freak like me or one of those sleek, modern people, take the time to enjoy and even bask in the beauty all around you. It will refresh your soul! And we all know what He thinks about home interiors and housewares. Don't even get me started. Remember God designed the details of Solomon's amazing, lavish, over-the-top temple, but that's a topic for another day!

Cake in the Oven

ONCE A WOMAN WANTS TO become pregnant, every unsuccessful month seems like a job interview without a job offer. You stir up your optimism. You consult the internet and employ every old wives' tale you've ever heard. You bully your husband, and at the end of the unsuccessful month, you have a grief-filled tantrum.

It took us three years to conceive my son, David. About two years later, I begged the Lord for that second baby. Rachel told Jacob in the book of Genesis, "Give me children, or I'll die!" (30:12 NIV). Sounds familiar.

I beat on my husband, Karl, for eight years before he agreed to adopt my daughter, Lily. It was a total of ten years before I conceived a second time. Well, that's not strictly true; I miscarried twice before she was born. My second daughter I named Grace. During those years, I was completely sympathetic of the heathen women who worshipped fertility gods, and was tempted actually to join them. (Just kidding)Back in those days, the church I attended was filled with happy, homeschooling women who gave birth every spring. They shared maternity clothes and had preschool co-ops, play dates, and generally enjoyed a big family sorority. I forfeited my peace and joy on a regular basis, and rather than enjoying the little family I had, I turned a million shades of envious green. I was jealous of their mini-vans, their noisy dinners, their chaotic Christmases, even their sibling rivalry sounded attractive.

I dragged Karl to an infertility specialist where we both suffered through a battery of uncomfortable, undignified tests. They were inconclusive, and my infertility was shrouded in mystery.

I went on pills, graduated to shots, moved on to surgery. My life revolved around blood work and ultrasound technology. On two different occasions, I was pregnant for a few weeks, and sadly both ended. Tons of people were devastated on my behalf.

At the same time, my self-pitying, one-track mind probably made me difficult to have as a friend. My pastor's wife, while praying for me, had the courage to ask me if I'd ever considered that this might be an idol in my life.

"That's ridiculous!" I replied. In my heart, I knew she was right. I had set up a shrine in my heart to the idea of being pregnant. God and I had this pattern where I'd have a tantrum every month, be mad at Him, pout, then repent, and worship, because in the end,He's the only real source of comfort anyway.

My wise husband had a brainwave, "You should go to graduate school."

Me: "I don't want to go to graduate school. I want more kids."

Karl: "I really think it would be good for you to be successful at another endeavor. I feel pretty strongly about this. It would give you permanent teaching certification. You're going."

Karl made the appointment, drove me to registration, and

wrote the check. Boom! I attended Nazareth College part-time for four years and added a TESOL certification and a Master's degree in education to my résumé.

The graduate work was healing for me. I loved the classes, loved the homework, loved the new people I was meeting. Teaching English to internationals was something I had done as a volunteer; it was exciting to study the more technical side of language acquisition. Emotionally, the sun hadn't come out yet, but it had stopped raining, and the days seemed brighter.

After I graduated from Nazareth College, Karl said, "I just thought you'd get pregnant during the graduate school. I think we should investigate adoption." So, we began the process of adoptive lawyers, home studies, and info nights at adoption agencies and crisis pregnancy centers. We even had a separate phone line installed for prospective birth moms. We sold our little ranch and bought a bigger house. We started to feel prayerfully expectant, kind of like being pregnant emotionally.

It was late the following spring when we received a phone call from a crisis pregnancy ministry concerning a birth-mom who wanted to know more about us. She had initially been attracted to our letters of inquiry.

"When is the baby due?" I asked the director of the ministry.

"Saturday," was her response.

Lily was actually born the following Thursday, and then we brought her home that Saturday.

Proverbs 13:12 says, "Longing fulfilled is a tree of life" (NIV). That's true.

When David held Lily for the first time, he said, "I've been praying for this baby for my whole life!" I guess that's how it seemed to him.

Nine months later, lo and behold, I turned up pregnant with Grace, which felt like a full quiver to me.

Looking back, the Lord was faithful to me. I wish I hadn't wasted all that time in self-pity and unbelief. I wish I had bought a mini-van sooner. If I had to tell anyone how I would handle that situation again, I would say that God isn't like some bad Father who's asleep on the couch on your behalf. He's preparing something amazing. Hating the process is draining and depressing. Your heavenly Father actually has your family portrait framed on His desk. He is in the process of answering your prayer. He's a good, good Father.

Season to Taste

O NCE UPON A TIME, IN a neighborhood not far away, a frazzled mother of a little girl with disabilities wrung her hands together as she and her child's pediatrician discussed putting her daughter on ADHD medication. You see, somewhere in her idealized, fairytale brain, the young mother had the idea that if she were loving, wise, and disciplined enough, her daughter would be somewhat perfect. People would say of her children, "Everyone needs a Savior, but with her kids it's hard to know why; they're just so virtuous."

Poof! Then, I woke up.

The truth is that self-control is lovely if it's within your reach, but this child seemed to need a little more help. Strategies and structure just weren't enough. Frankly, it was a matter of her safety. For me, the young mom of our story, giving her the meds that were prescribed seemed like selling out my desire to see the miraculous.

I imagined my faith-filled friends saying, "God can heal her; pray harder. She needs a strict diet with no colors, sugars, or flavors!"

Then, like wisdom from another realm, my doctor said, "You know, if you try them and you don't like the results, we can just take her off the meds."

Wow! That was so freeing. As it turned out, the doctor's advice became a guiding principle for me to transfer into all different aspects of my parenting and my marriage and my adulthood. "Try it. If you don't like it, you can stop."

That's such a freeing way to look at all kinds of stuff—lessons, jobs, medications, teams, you name it. Don't be afraid; make adjustments. You don't have to know in advance if it's a good system. Try it.

As it turned out, the meds gave my daughter the mental and emotional margins to make good choices. The change was so dramatic that teachers noticed immediately. "Whatever you're doing at home seems to be working. Keep it up." That breakthrough was like a revelation. It made me wish I had made the decision sooner.

What other areas of my life could be improved by venturing to make a change if I wasn't so afraid of making mistakes? Here's the thing that I learned: Not only is the powerful God on my side, but He isn't hiding His will or provision from me. He is a disclosing God. He's leading me. We just need to remember that if we venture out, and we make a mistake, most things can be adjusted. What a relief!

You Take the Cake

T HE MOST INCREDIBLE PART ABOUT the story of Joseph in Genesis is how he behaved when no one was looking. He had no pastor, no Bible, no cool worship music, no close-knit small group; he didn't even have any groovy podcasts.

What made Joseph, well, Joseph? I mean, he was born handsome and intelligent. Those were gifts, but what made him insightful, helpful, and honorable? The same sensitivity that enabled him to solve other people's problems could have made him self-absorbed and brooding. Joseph could have easily been incapacitated by bitterness. After all, his brothers sold him!

My friend, Bob Sorge, says the distinctive factor in Joseph's life was that he was raised by Jacob, who had wrestled with the angel and had his name changed to Israel. It was later in his transformed life that Jacob became the adoring dad of Joseph, who was born to his beloved Rachel.

We know Rachel wanted that baby so badly she could taste it.

Joseph was the son of two adoring parents. Remember, his father was so captivated by him that he had a special coat made for Joseph. I can picture Jacob teaching his little prince everything he knew and then showering him with admiration. "Yes, that's the right answer! How smart you are! You're my boy! You take the cake!"

Maybe the secret is having an adoring, approving Father. Jesus had an adoring, approving Father. "This is my beloved Son, in whom I am well pleased!" is what God said on the day that Jesus was baptized by John the Baptist. Jesus knew who He was, and still the Father took the time to tell Him in front of other people, "This is my beloved Son, in whom I am well pleased; listen to Him" (Matt 17:5).

As far as you and I are concerned, knowing that we have our identity rooted in being in Christ makes it so that we too enjoy the approval of our heavenly Father. I don't need to react out of fear or shame. My heavenly Father is not withholding good things from me. Like Old Testament Joseph, I can respond out of my conviction that I am about my Father's business even when I am in a secluded, obscure, or anonymous place. The Holy Spirit can sensitize my conscience to what He needs to have said and done.

Maybe the best training I can give to my own children is to teach them that their heavenly Father approves of them. I can encourage them to enjoy God's presence and favor even when they find themselves in obscurity, seclusion, or possibly an unplanned pit.

Risky Recipes

J ESUS GOES TO UNBELIEVABLE LENGTHS to get us to lay aside our fears. He wants us to look at who He is and what He wants, and then go and do amazing exploits. These days there seems to be a groundswell of people who want me to mobilize, to go into uncharted waters, and to be brave. Is this just happening to me, or is this a major trend like the Ice Bucket Challenge?

In John 14:1, Jesus says: "Believe in, adhere to, trust in and rely on Me" (AMP). Then, in verses 12 and 13, He says that those who believe in Him will do the works He did and do "greater works" than He did. Finally, in verse 17, Jesus makes reference to the coming of the Holy Spirit, saying, "He lives within you and will be with you," and He "will teach you all things." So, bottom line, there isn't any reason for you or me to be afraid to dream or be brave. God will go before us, and He will answer our prayers.

I had to ask myself what it is, then, that holds me back from taking on new frontiers. You know what I came up with?

I'm afraid of looking stupid. Mostly, I'm inhibited by the cynical voice in my own head that has been constraining me for too long. *What if I look like an idiot?*

Yikes! While sharp and biting are good words when describing cheese, they are not useful in our minds or mouths. The mocking voice in my mind is not the voice of the Holy Spirit who wants me to be brave; it's the voice of my own fear of making a fool out of myself. You know what, though? I'm getting a little bored with that line of thinking. Lately, I'm starting to conclude that guarding my dignity is overrated. After all, what have I got to lose other than my pride?

The secret to all of this is found at the beginning of John 14, "Believe, trust, and rely on Me," Jesus said. To do that, I have to fix the eyes of my heart and mind on Jesus. As I focus on Him and His glory, my looking foolish becomes way less important.

When it comes to being brave, as a mom, my babies' safety always made me more courageous than I had been before. For example, bees and wasps might have sent me running before my babies were born, but when one dared to buzz by my babies, it just made me mad! "Get away from my babies, you vile thing!" The fear was swallowed up by a bigger priority, protecting my babies.

Jesus says that the Holy Spirit is my Teacher, Helper, and Counselor. He is going to guide me. That's a good deal. When we take time to look and listen to the Lord, He gives us vision that can eclipse our fears. He gives us vision that propels us to do the "greater works" that He has in mind for us to do!

Cake Toppers

THERE'S A GROOVY BAKERY IN a hipster neighborhood near where I live that produces cakes that would make anyone swoon. Just thinking about these cakes makes me drool. Their Instagram feed has over twelve thousand people gawking at their artwork. The buttercream flowers look like live floral arrangements, and the flavor choices of the fillings and frostings will make you glad you were born—mocha, gooey caramel, dark chocolate—so much creativity and skill!

You know what it makes me wonder? *What came before the bakery? How long have these girls been baking? Where did they learn? Who ate all the mistakes?* (Just kidding.)

But seriously, I marvel at people who dare to take risks, and I wonder what kind of playpen they grew up in. Were their parents and friends adoring and affirming? Brave and cavalier? Or, did they do exploits in spite of the fact that they grew up among pessimists and cynics?

I want to create an atmosphere of bravery at my house, so I'm declaring war on mindsets like: fear of failure, performance anxiety, and the phobia of looking stupid. I'm going to foster this mentality instead: What's the worst thing that could happen? Did you enjoy yourself? Were you a blessing? Keep going!

In the Garden of Eden, there were two trees: the Tree of the Knowledge of Good and Evil, and the Tree of Life. Adam and Eve weren't supposed to eat of the first one, but they could eat from the Tree of Life. Although the privilege of eating from the Tree of Life was lost after Adam and Eve disobeyed God, I believe God wants to restore us to be people with access to life, health, and bravery. Jesus came so that we may live a life of grace and abundance.

Proverbs 13:12 says, "Hope deferred makes the heart sick, but longing fulfilled is a tree of life" (NIV). When God puts a dream in your heart and then that dream comes to pass, Scripture says that is a "Tree of Life" moment.

Revelation 2:7 says, "To the one who is victorious, I will give the right to eat from the tree of life, which is in the paradise of God" (NIV). This verse is referring to heaven. There, we will have access to the Tree of Life if we don't give up, but instead we overcome.

For me, I'm asking God to apply His "on earth as it is in heaven" principle from the prayer He taught His disciples to pray (Matt 6:10 ESV). I'm asking Him for a foretaste of this heavenly abundance here and now.

The Tree of Life represents living with possibilities, creativity, bravery, and favor. What cool endeavors can we foster in our own lives and in those around us when we are breathing in this heavenly oxygen? Baking cakes is only the beginning!

Proofing Dough

I HAD THIS WEIRD EXPERIENCE WHERE I woke up in the middle of the night and changed out of what I had worn to bed and put on my favorite night shirt, which is simply an over-sized T-shirt. What I wore to bed initially had way too much tight elastic. At the time, I didn't think I'd care. I ended up in what I call my "pet shirt." Bliss.

Am I the only one? Is that weird?

I also have a pair of black fleece pants I wear from November through March. I call them my "pet pants." I even invented a verb which describes coming home after a long day and putting on cozy clothes— "Fleece Out."

So, when someone asks me, "Are you going out with us?"

"No, I'm gonna go home and fleece out."

(Fleecing out, by the way, also involves eating something yummy and comforting while watching anything on the Travel Channel.)

It's strange how we have preferences and patterns. When my

daughter was little, she was diagnosed with a sensory integration disorder, which means how things smelled, sounded, felt, and tasted were super-amplified for her so she wouldn't wear anything with a tag or a seam she could feel, not even socks. And she hated loud noises. It made life interesting. You know what helped me accept her limitations? I realized that I had a ton of my own preferences about feels, smells, and tastes.

I think it's good to have preferences. It's what makes us individuals. The problem comes when life requires us to be flexible because stuff happens beyond our control. We must flex when what we've become attached to becomes unavailable.

I hate that. It's especially tricky when it comes to people. Sometimes, the very person who God sent to make provision for me in an area, like a pastor, a doctor, a teacher or a friend, is no longer able to provide for me. It may be that they've retired, moved away, or passed away. God is asking me to be flexible about where He makes provision. He's asking me to trust Him, and that's hard.

Here's the thing: Training wheels on your bike are great for a season, but eventually, they're actually a hindrance to your riding with freedom. He wants us to be free. The same God who sent those supports, sometimes wants us to rely on Him for what we used to get from others. Maybe He's asking us to make a new friend or try a new dentist or make a new pattern. This is my current challenge, being adaptable. Maybe this is just an indication that I'm continuing to grow.

Trying a New Recipe

I T SEEMS LIKE GOD ALWAYS raises up pioneers to go and do the things that others find daunting. In the Old Testament, Jeremiah prophesied that after the Jews endured seventy years of captivity, God would stir the heart of the king to rebuild the house of the Lord in Jerusalem. In the book of Ezra, we read about Cyrus, the king of Persia, who was stirred by the Spirit of the Lord to make this proclamation: Whoever, of the exiled Jews, wants to go rebuild the temple in Jerusalem, should go.

Cyrus then brought out of the treasury all the gold and silver that had been taken from Solomon's original temple in Jerusalem. He sent it with God's people to go rebuild the temple (see Ezra 2).

It sounds like it would have been a pretty intimidating task, going back on foot from Persia to Jerusalem, clearing the rubble, and building the temple again. Some of the Jews didn't go, though. They stayed in Babylon. Maybe they had already opened a kosher deli, a law firm, or a chain of jewelry stores; maybe the idea of starting over was too much for them.

Here we are in the year 2017 tempted to dread. The election was confusing, and the outcome interesting. (I guess that was the safest word to use.) We are told that the health care system is a mess. We see devastation all over the world, the effect of natural disasters like floods and tornados. We are told there are no jobs. Violence in some U.S. urban areas is out of control. The list goes on. We can be paralyzed by the tragedy all around us.

When I was young, the war in Viet Nam was an ongoing nightmare. Nixon was impeached. Carter won the presidency only to ration gas at the pump—talk about low national morale! We still thought communism was a big global threat; we thought it was the end of life as we knew it. We weren't even out of our teens!

It's easy to love innovation and best case scenarios at the beginning of adulthood. In every generation, there is a temptation for our optimism to leave with our muscle tone.

Little by little, methods change, styles change, societal norms shift. Think about it. Phone booths, tape players, and soap dishes have all been replaced by better inventions. The challenge is always to be brave enough to see opportunity in the trial of change. It seems like in every generation there are those who are excited to embrace the challenge and to fearlessly meet it with a wry grin and a new idea. This, perhaps, is a type of giftedness which is irrespective of intellect or social status—a gift for being able to adapt to change. I think someone with this gift is called a pioneer.

We as people of God have an advantage. We are in relationship with the Giver of every good and perfect gift. He is the one with the new solution, the new recipe. I want to be that kind of person—one whose faith makes me optimistic, not bugged when systems change.

Lord, help me look and listen to You. When a new solution is called for, help me not to dig in my heels and pine for the old. Make me a new wineskin that's flexible (see Matt 9:17), *believing that You are never without provision and a plan that would benefit me.*

Help! My Cake's Fallen, and It Can't Get Up!

IN 2 KINGS 4, WE read about a kindhearted lady, the Shunammite. She had no children, and rather than being depressed or obsessed with her situation (which I know from experience can feel like prolonged unemployment), she chose to bless the prophet, Elisha. She built him his own guest room so that he could rest whenever he passed through town.

Elisha was so moved by her efforts for him that he sought to thank her, and indeed he interceded to God for her. As a result, she bore a son. She was thrilled.

A few years later, the child was out in the field with his dad when he complained of head pain and shortly thereafter died on his mother's lap. She proceeded to go to find Elisha. "Did I ask for a son from my lord? Did I not say, Do not give me false hope?" (2 Kgs 4:28 AMP).

Translation: "The son you helped me have is now dead."

Elisha tried to send his servant to heal the boy, but the mother refused to leave Elisha's side until he came with her. Elisha ended up going to the lad and lying on top of him not once, but twice. The Bible says, they were mouth to mouth, eye to eye, and hand to hand. He warmed the boy with his own body (see 2 Kgs 4:34–37). He got up, stretched, and then he did it again. Presently, the boy had a sneezing fit, opened his eyes, and was restored to his adoring momma.

Here's the takeaway for me: The Lord gives you an amazing vision or dream. It could be of a marriage or a child. It could be a ministry, a business, or a relationship. It might even be a big, amazing endeavor! Your ambition is from God, but over time, that thing starts to die. In fact, it's dead. Perhaps the Lord is asking you to speak life into your dream, even if it ends up costing you in ways that you never imagined.

It's time to act like Elisha. You put your eyes on that dead dream. You fan the vision. You focus on it and muse on the matter. Your eyes are looking for how God's plan might unfold. You put your mouth on it. You speak positively into the situation, and you talk to people who can help or direct you. And lastly, you put your hands on the thing which speaks of your applying yourself to the matter. And you do so unswervingly, working harder than you ever imagined, contending for the dream.

But be prepared. Other people will tell you concerning the dream God gave you, "It's too late. You're too old." After all, isn't it against ceremonial law to hang out on a dead thing? Gross.

Don't be surprised if you get tired and are tempted to walk away. God says to persevere in the situation because He will bring the miracle of regeneration through your touch, your body, and your mouth. You carry the miraculous—just like Elisha. Sometimes, it only takes a particular brand of stubbornness.

God alone has the power to resurrect the dead, and in the end of this story, God showed up and rewarded the faith-filled tenacity of the Shunamite. Elisha said to her, "Pick up your son" (2 Kgs 4:36). And the great news is she left worshipping with her miracle boy holding her hand.

Timing is Everything

Today, I was reading in 1 Kings about the beginning of Solomon's glorious reign. I read that Solomon offered sacrifices at Gibeon as was the custom of his father, David. Solomon offered sacrifices there, and then later that night, the Lord appeared to him and said, "Ask what I shall give you" (3:5).

Solomon went on to ask for an understanding mind to lead the people. He asked for wisdom, which is the appropriation of knowledge.

God was pleased and promised to honor Solomon's desire and to also bless him with riches, honor, and long life. Cool, right?

The thing that struck me as odd was this: The high places where Israel's leaders sacrificed, that later made God so angry, were the right places to make the sacrifices at the beginning of the nation's history.

Joshua and Samuel both offered sacrifices in places like Shiloh and Gilgal. It wasn't until David brought the ark of the covenant into Jerusalem that the city of Jerusalem was considered a place of worship. Solomon was the one who finally built a glorious building, the temple, to house the ark of the covenant in a fixed location. Before Solomon built the temple, sacrificial worship happened in the wilderness, at the tabernacle (in a tent), or on a hilltop.

The issue for me is this: What used to be the right thing to do became the wrong thing to do. People changed the nature of the sacrifices from ones that honored God to ones that honored idols like Baal and Asherim. We later read, "In every city of Judah, [Ahaz] made high places to make offerings to other gods, provoking the anger of the Lord, the God of his fathers" (2 Chron 28:25 NASB).

What used to be the right thing to do became the wrong thing. At first, it was subtle—right sacrifice, wrong place—and then more obvious the wrong sacrifice at wrong place.

Seems to be that disobeying what we know to be spiritual disciplines—like gathering together to worship, or tithing, or being in prayer, or reading our Bibles—can begin innocently but can become more dangerous over time.

For me, once my son got married, it was no longer my responsibility to watch over him and to look after him. I needed to let go of what I had held onto so tightly. Sounds silly, but I'm learning that sometimes even good patterns need to change.

God requires something new from us. Jesus said that new wine requires new wineskins (see Mark 2:22).

In order for us to grab onto the new thing, perhaps we need to let go of the old thing, something that used to enrich our lives, like a job or a friendship. Conversely, priorities like our time in prayer may increase as does our giving.

Sometimes, we don't end up looking balanced. Following God's call can leave us looking a little weird.

When it comes to worship, the unique feature of a move of the

Spirit can, over time, become stale and mechanical. We want the habits and patterns of our lives to honor God. We want to promote spiritual growth in our own lives and in the lives of those we love. I suggest we allow God to go through our spiritual closets and give Him the liberty to help us "weed out" what is no longer "in style" as far as He's concerned. We need to let God look at how we spend our time and our money, and with whom we spend it. We need to let God speak to us about our attitudes and eating habits, and what we do for fun and for ministry.

New wine sometimes involves new methods or landscape. It can be scary. Sometimes, you feel like a novice again, threatened and unsure of the right thing to do. New wine leans not on its own understanding. New wine means the loser doesn't get what he deserves; rather, he gets a fresh start, another chance.

I think that being legalistic and judgmental are occupational hazards of becoming a mature disciple of Christ. It's kind of like getting plaque on your teeth is inevitable for people who eat. There's only one solution—regular maintenance.

I want to be transformed so that my years walking with Jesus don't make me into someone who's fossilized in my attitudes but responsive to the needs of the Master. Being alone with Jesus is the only way to keep pride, unbelief, and legalism from taking root and becoming major problems. His voice, His Word, and the power of the Holy Spirit persuade me to repent of my bad attitudes and impure motives.

When I look back on the story of the prodigal, the elder sibling, and the Father, I realize that for all the time on the father's farm, the older one never took the time to be in the father's company; he never learned to take the time to learn the real family business which involved love, forgiveness, and redemption.

Maturing is fraught with pitfalls like fossilized perspectives, painful experiences, and antiquated teaching. These mindsets that we have put into place as a natural consequence for having lived sometimes trip us up. Unconsciously, we invent policies to protect ourselves from future pain.

At the same time, there are some advantages to having walked in faith for longer than the most recent model of the iPhone has been on the market. I can lean confidently on the following truth: God is good, and He cares for me and the details of my life. Having your heart broken is inevitable, if your heart is beating. It's okay.

The Virgin Mary asked of the angel, Gabriel, "Yes, but how?" So, that's what I'll take for my own. I'll say *yes* to God even when I don't understand His reasons or methods.

Lord, I'm asking you for a renewed wineskin. I know You are sending new wine. The new wine is divine perspective, supernatural thinking, fresh grace, and new mercy. God, I give you permission to rearrange my thought processes.

Grease the Pan

RECENTLY, I WAS PREPARING TO speak at a gathering. As I began to think about what I could share with a group of women that I hadn't yet met, the two things that came to me were that women universally need to be flexible and generous. What do you think?

I don't know anyone who isn't being called upon to graciously accept change. If you're good at school, graduating makes you leave that community and go to a job in a new setting with new people or no people. If you have been working, perhaps you have experienced a job change or have been laid off. Or maybe you're having a baby and having to decide whether to stay home, or how work will look after the baby comes. Or, maybe you're like my friends and I who had stayed at home for years but now are going back to work. The maid doesn't live in our houses anymore. (I sure do miss her!)

And we mustn't forget our children. They leave. They come back, and they come back with kids of their own. My girlfriend told me that her grandsons were sabotaging her diet because of all the snacks, Happy Meals, and Chicken Nuggets.

Oh, and we can't forget husbands. Husbands have to be loved in a whole lot of different ways. A woman with whom I was very close, lost her husband Sunday. That's some serious change.

Every time we think we've got it down, the mode of operation changes. Sometimes, it's all brand new, and sometimes, the avocado color comes back into style! We need to remain flexible, and there's a secret to it: being motivated by love. It greases everything. The oil of love makes old leather soft! For the sake of love, old dogs do new tricks.

I can't speak for you, but let me tell you something: I don't want to be flexible!! I liked it the old way!! I want to let out one long cry, "Why???"

Jesus said, "Don't put new wine in old wineskins" (Matt 9:17). You know why? Because new ideas, wonderful trends, gifts, and inventions need to be in flexible containers. And love is the necessary emollient for our hearts as it motivates us and softens us so that we can hold the new. The apostle Peter clarifies this for us. He said:

> Stay wide-awake in prayer. Most of all, love each other as if your life depended on it. Love makes up for practically anything. Be quick to give a meal to the hungry or a bed to the homeless—cheerfully. Be generous with the different things God gave you, pass them around so that all get in on it: if words, let it be God's words; if help, let it be God's hearty help. That way, God's bright presence will be evident in everything through Jesus, and he'll get all the credit as the One mighty in everything—encores to the end of time. (1 Pet 4:7—11 MSG)

That's powerful advice to the church, but it's easier said than done. It's very difficult for us to give when we feel like there's no more where that came from! It's difficult to be loving at all when there's stress in our families or at our jobs, or when all kinds of news out in the world suck up our joy. How do we get generosity of spirit to give again?

We spend time alone with God and His Word, and then something phenomenal happens. He pours mother-strength into us so that we can pour it out again. He reveals intimate details to us about ourselves and about His nature through His Word. He calls us to be alone with Him to refresh us, and then we can go out and do loving tasks on His behalf! That's what He did with the disciples in Mark 6. He called them aside to be refreshed and then reinvigorated. That's way cooler than feeling like a group home worker who works all three shifts all seven days! That's way cooler than feeling like a scullery maid who's relegated to the kitchen and the laundry room as a lifelong sentence.

I serve, but He refreshes me because I serve Him.

Trust me. We all get bad-tempered when we feel like we're being asked to give what we don't have in the areas of:

- stamina,
- privacy,
- patience,
- provision,
- finances,
- kindness,
- time,
- ideas, or
- food.

Sometimes, when I'm mad at my kids, I yell, "You can't have my other kidney! I've given you all I can give! I'm so done! If I wasn't looking forward to grandchildren, I'd strangle you!" (Of course, this is usually late at night when someone wants an emergency, school-related crisis run to the store. I'm a sucker for school-related emergencies like craft supplies for a project, or a white shirt for a choral concert.)

But other times, when I'm tuned and plugged in to the Source of good gifts, I can be big-hearted, magnanimous, patient, creative, and generous with other people—even my own children.

At such times, I feel His favor. I'm not threatened by other women who are younger, smarter, and thinner, or who have better behaved kids than mine. I can get by with less for me: less privacy, less sleep, less attention.

Trust the Lord for the grace to grow, adapt, and accept change. Then, we women will see God move in our lives, marriages, families, churches, schools, communities, and world. As we open ourselves to receive His love in the first place, in order to be effective daughters of the Most High God, we can go out and rock our world!

Part 3: Delivering Cakes

Special Delivery

WHEN THE BOOK OF EXODUS opens, Joseph, the darling of the Egyptians and the Israelites, has been dead for a long time. The people of Israel have become numerous and powerful, and thus, a threat to the Pharaoh. So, he decided to place heavy burdens on them and to make them slaves who were pressed into oppressive manual labor. The Israelites were forced to do all kinds of work in the field and work with mortar and brick. "So," we are told, "they ruthlessly made the people of Israel work as slaves" (Exod 1:14).

What's worse than that? The order Pharaoh gave two Hebrew midwives, one named Shiphrah and the other Puah. (Bet you don't see those names on key chains on the rack in the souvenir shop on the thruway.) He told the midwives, "When you serve as midwife to the Hebrew women and see them on the birthstool, if it is a son, you shall kill him, but if it is a daughter, she shall live. When you serve as a midwife to the Hebrew women, if you see that she's having a son, then kill him, but if it is a daughter, let her live" (Exod 1:16). Yeesh! Can you imagine? But the next part I love!

"But the midwives feared God and did not do as the king of Egypt commanded them, but let the male children live" (Exod 1:17).

So, the Pharaoh was furious. He called the midwives to appear before him and asked them why they didn't obey his command.

"Oh, King," the girls answered, "the Hebrew women are not like Egyptian women; they are vigorous and give birth before the midwives arrive" (Exod 1:19 NIV). The Scripture says, "So God was kind to the midwives and the people increased and became even more numerous. And because the midwives feared God, he gave them families of their own" (Exod 1:20-21 NIV). God honored their bravery.

Jochabed was a Levite woman who gave birth to one of those baby boys. His name was Moses. When she saw how beautiful he was, she hid him instead of throwing him in the Nile. Mothering a beautiful baby makes you brave.

When Moses got too big to hide, Jochabed made a sea-worthy cradle for her son and floated him in the Nile, deputizing his sister, Miriam, to watch over him. Ultimately, Pharaoh's daughter and her girls found the floating baby in the cattails. Miriam volunteered to go find a woman who could nurse the baby. (Surprise!) Jochabed got to nurse her own son!

The real story is this: Before Moses can grow up to redeem his people, a whole team of brave women are raised up by God to defy the enemy and redeem Moses! Redemption is still on the heart of God. That's still his primary business. He still uses mothers, sisters, single women, old and young. In ages past, God used brave women to accomplish His will, and it's what He does today. What God wants us to do is listen to Him and be valiant!

Wrapped in Spices

PHARISEE IS A WORD WITH a bad connotation. To be pharisaical is to be more concerned with the rules and not necessarily the well-being of any individual person. However, there were a couple exceptions—Pharisees who didn't completely fit the definition. These were those who benefitted from the P.R.A—the Pharisee Recovery Act. The most obvious example was the apostle Paul, the murder accomplice who, after being roughed up by his horse, a blinding light, and an audible voice, cried out to God and was transformed. Pretty dramatic.

There was another guy whose story is a little lesser known. He wasn't very brave. He came to Jesus at night because he was afraid of his superiors. Nicodemus was a Pharisee who jeopardized his position of honor to seek out Jesus and find out the truth. You get the idea that, when he saw Jesus speaking in public, he knew he needed to know the whole truth about who Jesus actually was, so he made an appointment to talk to Him in private.

When Jesus explained the exact nature of faith to Nicodemus, he believed, and eventually, he was transformed. He became both merciful and brave. He defended Jesus to the High Priest, saying, "Can a man be crucified without a trial?" Ultimately, Nicodemus, along with his friend Joseph of Arimathea, asked Pilate for permission to take Jesus' body down from the cross and bury it after the crucifixion. The hotshot disciples were hiding by this time and were nowhere to be found. The only ones with faith at that point were these two men and the women who were grieving.

Here's the most amazing thing: Maybe people who are dutiful, conscientious, and faithful are not the first to initiate risky behaviors. They are not always perceived as brave or valiant. Perhaps they never get to be known as swashbuckling or cavalier. They do, however reluctant, do the right thing once they are persuaded what that looks like. These are responsible types who hold the bag for other people. They are motivated by tenderheartedness or mercy.

Nicodemus and Joseph of Arimathea were brave enough to petition Pilate for the body of Jesus after He was crucified. After taking His body down from the cross, they wrapped it in linen with spices and placed it in Joseph's expensive, unused tomb. It's interesting to note the body was put to death at the order of the other religious rulers in charge at the time who were Nic's co-workers and bosses.

I can only imagine what the reaction of the resurrected Jesus was once He met Nicodemus and Joseph face to face. I don't know if it was in Jerusalem or in heaven. I only know that being thanked at that moment by the Lord Jesus would be amazing. "Thank you, Nicodemus and Joseph. What would I have done without you? You both were so brave. I appreciate you so much!"

That encounter, the one with the reluctant, obscure guy, makes me happy. It assures me that not all heroes are the most likely candidates. Sometimes, the hero is the person with the sensitive conscience, who does the right thing with a nervous stomach and sweaty palms. That's the guy or girl who sometimes makes history.

Not Exactly Peaches and Cream

Y OU GOT TO LIKE RUTH. You know what I like about Ruth?
She wasn't passive in the very least. In general, when I think of
those ancient cultures, I think of women who were either living in
a tent or in a village, basically preoccupied with tending to children
and sheep. Not Ruth.

Ruth was married to Naomi's son, Mahlon, not from her family,
a foreigner in Moab, a little controversial. She braved widowhood
and came away clinging to the faith of her in-laws. This was not
the path of least resistance. Ruth left town with Naomi instead of
returning to her mom and dad, not the norm. At every turn, Ruth
took a risk. I love that.

Naomi took Ruth back to her hometown. She introduced Ruth
around and got Ruth a job picking barley in the fields of a man
named Boaz, an older dude.

Ruth went out to glean in the fields belonging to Boaz because she and Naomi were poor and hungry, but Ruth kept her eyes open and her lipstick handy. Well, maybe she didn't wear lipstick, but I bet she was aware of what was happening around her. I bet part of her beauty was her purposeful bravery.

Soon Boaz and Ruth had a brief encounter out in the field, the kind that usually happens in chapter three of a romance novel. I think she wanted Boaz. Naomi approved. Maybe Naomi sensed God's favor and was sure that God had a plan.

One night after Ruth had finished with her farm work, she got cleaned up the way girls do. It was harvest time. She waited until Boaz was fed and in a good mood (smart girl). She went to him and entreated him to cover her. He did. Ultimately, he married her.

The Bible says he redeemed her. Sigh. That's so beautiful. In the end, God chose to include Ruth in the lineage of Jesus. She bore Obed, the grandfather of David!

I love Ruth because she was brave. She was persuaded that faith in God was her only recourse. She got knocked down, and she got back up. She kept moving, believing, listening, trusting, and acting. Ruth wasn't preoccupied with what other people thought or said. She didn't spend her time entertaining worst case scenarios. She wasn't paralyzed by doubt, fear, and dread. She could have been like her sister-in-law, Orpah, who went back to her own family when calamity struck. But nope, not Ruth.

I want to be brave and believe that God is good and that He is with me and that He is for me. I want to act, trusting that God's favor will guide me.

Sweet and Spicy

I T'S NOT UNCOMMON TO SEE a married couple who are made up of a dynamic, talented, fearless man and a supportive, competent woman. Those couples are everywhere—on television, in politics, in business, and especially in local churches.

He's flamboyant; she's grounded. There is, however, another model: women who have ideas, dreams, and drive, married to men who are secure enough to partner with them to facilitate their dreams. I call these men *flagpoles*.

These guys are married to women who are colorful extroverts, and that suits them just fine. They like their *flag* women. Her skill set is attractive to him. She's sweet and spicy, and he likes it. He doesn't feel the need to compete with her, let alone diminish her. He's a stable guy who likes to think of ways to make her ideas happen. He's a facilitator, a producer.

I also think the stress we put on our love-relationships is often related to not just our dreams, but to the rate at which we achieve them. I've seen young couples who are in a hurry to find the professional jobs of their dreams, start businesses or charities, finish their graduate degrees, buy houses and dogs, and have children all within the first few years of their marriage. The dreams are really good; it's just how fast we expect them can kill us. Be patient.

Maybe the new definition of love is finding someone who has vision to see you become, and the faith and patience to believe, what God had in mind for the two of you from the very beginning.

Cupcake, Anyone?

WHAT IF THE PRODIGAL IN the parable had been a daughter? What would that have looked like? What if the elder sibling was a sister? What would she have sounded like? What would we have called the story, "Prodigal Girls and Their Legalistic Sisters"? That sounds like a new show on cable.

The elder sibling in the biblical parable was a guy who had consistently worked hard and had no intention of sharing what was left of the estate with Junior. After all, Junior blew through 50 percent of the original plantation. That's a lot.

If the eldest were a sister, she would have been judgmental, performance-driven, territorial with a shrew-quality reserved for bad tempered women; in other words, she would have been considered a word that rhymes with witch.

I know. I've been there. I've vied for intimacy with other women while remaining fiercely territorial myself. Competitive, overworked, and perpetually annoyed, yeah, I've been there and done that, too. I've held standards for younger women in the faith that I myself could never live up to.

Why is it when a girl gives away her purity there's no turning back? Why is that?

A girl, well, if she has a wild past, gets treated like yesterday's leftover birthday cake. (A guy, on the other hand, can sow wild oats, live crazy, and respond to an altar call only to be made the youth leader. Cool ink on his arm is part of his testimony.)

She needs to pay her dues. It serves her right. I'm not surprised. What did you expect from a family like that? These unlovely, un-grace-filled, non-fragrant sentiments have actually gone through my mind. These mean-spirited, unloving judgmental thoughts are not reserved for any specific generation either. I've heard deadly words come out of high-school girls and grey-haired women.

Jesus told the Parable of the Prodigal Son for the faith-filled and the faith-fallen so both would understand about giving and receiving grace. Jesus locked horns with the Pharisees because He knew they made obstacles between people and the Father. They set up obstacle courses to keep faith from being simple and accessible. Do I do that?

Dear God, help me to pave a fragrant way to Your doorstep so that others can come to You unhindered. May I better reflect Your loving embrace to those who are looking for love and acceptance. I choose to stop projecting my own bitterness and negative experiences on my unsuspecting sisters. I receive fresh grace for myself and them. Amen.

Cake and Ice Cream

THE IMPLICATION FOR THE OLDER brother in the story of the prodigal son is that all the provision for the party was always at his disposal. "Son, you are always with me, and all that is mine is yours" (Luke 15:31). The Father is more than willing to share the richness of His house with His children.

The question is this: What inhibits those of us who are the "elder sisters" in the house from knowing when to take the time, money, and energy to throw a good party? Is it our pride?

I think we don't understand how God thinks. He's not stingy; He's not in a bad mood. Maybe we don't understand how valuable it is to celebrate, laugh, feast, rest, and dance. If it was in the heart of the Father to gather friends and make a blow-out party, maybe we just have to get to know Him well enough to understand how He thinks, about His generosity, and grace. Perhaps it's our job to take the time to enjoy Him and His provision and to stop having an exaggerated opinion about how important our accomplishments are to God and to others.

Being loved by the Father, spending time appreciating and enjoying relationships He's provided, with food and music, being refreshed, may all be more important than we ever realized. Why is it so difficult for some of us to know how to celebrate? I'm asking God to show me what the culture of His Kingdom looks like as it pertains to a good party!

The Toothpick Test

Jesus prayed to the Father and said, "I have given them the glory you gave me, so they may be one even as we are one" (John 17:22 NLT).

Shazaam! What are the ramifications of that?! Jesus gives us glory? His glory? Jesus gives us his glory? He gives us His glory in order that we can showcase unity as Christians. That's crazy! Well, it must not be crazy because Jesus said it, but that must mean that our unity is very important to Him.

I've come to realize that walking in unity isn't really about our agreeing with each other. It's more about demonstrating supernatural love and humility. According to this passage, we're going to need glorious, wonder-working power in order to reflect the kind of oneness with one another that Jesus, the Holy Spirit, and the Father experience.

It's ironic because the longer you've been attending church, the more likely you are to see people's flaws and imperfections. Here's the type of thing you hear all the time:

- "Doesn't he even know he has blind spots in that area?"
- "How can she be so inconsistent?"
- "She's got pet ministries, pet peeves, and pet doctrines!"
- "Does he even read the New Testament?"

It doesn't take much insight to see weaknesses and frailty. Pointing out the frailty in others is not glorious or honorable; it's juvenile. Childish. You know what takes strength, what requires some maturity? Perceiving the shortcomings in others and choosing to cover their disabilities with your abilities.

I'm not talking about accommodating sin. I'm talking about tolerating frailty for the sake of love. We embrace the differences in one another, not expecting conformity. This is especially true when the weak place in another is a place of strength for you.

Here's an example. My tech friends help me when I'm helpless at technological problems. My math friends divide the check when we go out because I forget that there's a beverage, tax, and tip in addition to the salad I ate.

Sometimes, in local churches, it boils down to natural gifting, temperament, and preferences. I'm the go-to person when there's a need for someone who loves internationals, strangers, or crowds. They energize me.

The rest of the world sits up and takes notice when we care for each other and make provision for each other because that's when we reflect and reveal the love that Jesus talks about when He reflects the glory of the Father by doing His will.

Yes, Jesus values unity among us so much that He prayed for it on our behalf right before He went to the cross. He knows that, when we lock arms to do inspired work in the earth, mighty stuff gets done. Conversely, if we bicker, nothing gets accomplished. This is especially frustrating when arguments arise over issues that are really a matter of personal preferences like music style or territorial disputes.

Jesus realized that all this need for humility would require a boatload of supernatural assistance, so He sent us the Holy Spirit to guide us in these matters. I'm grateful that the prayer of Jesus for us was this: that His glory would be given to us so that we could become "perfectly united" as brothers and sisters, and that the world would see and know our love comes from Him.

Gluten Free

THESE DAYS MOST UPSCALE BAKERIES have gluten free and vegan options for their modern patrons. Back in the day, no one ever dreamed that we would need to accommodate and provide for the intersection between our health goals and our dessert dreams. You know what? Times change. Our collective understanding changes. You can be the first to embrace new ideas and information or you can be a late adapter, but the truth is, times change.

Similarly, some of our convictions can go through modification and change over time. Gray areas. I'm not talking about the essentials of faith or explicit sin. I'm talking about gray areas and our proneness to make them points of contention. As it turns out, it's nothing new. I was reading about Paul's opinion on circumcision. It seems to have transformed over time.

In Acts 16, Paul takes Timothy and has him circumcised because, while his mother was Jewish, his father was Greek and, apparently, Timothy had never been circumcised. This strikes me as odd because in Acts 15:10-19 Paul tells the Jerusalem Council that they should not require circumcision of gentiles. He advocated they abstain from sexual immorality, worshiping idols, and eating blood. (Sorry, no vampires allowed.)

Later, in Galatians 5:2-4, Paul strongly states to anyone who accepts circumcision, "Christ will be of no advantage to you … every man who accepts circumcision that he is obligated to keep the whole law. You are severed from Christ, you who would be justified by the law; you have fallen away from grace."

Isn't it curious how Paul's understanding matures over time? First, he observes the law, and then his inclination is to move away from it. Eventually, he moves to passionate conviction. There will be no circumcision!

Here's the takeaway: I need to be patient with myself and others who are constantly moving toward a more perfect understanding of the will and mind of God.

People's convictions are often shaped by their experiences, and I was not there when they experienced defining moments.

Tolerate young believers who are dogmatic about matters that might be a phase rather than a life message. Gently correct those whose thinking are unscriptural, especially in matters of grace and the law. Hang in there with those who interpret gray areas differently than you do.

Some people seem like specialists in certain areas about which they are especially passionate. That's okay. God gives some of us very specifics tasks.

So, we too must study, pray, and allow our perspectives to be adjusted by the Holy Spirit as He matures us and develops our convictions over time. We must allow room for others to learn, grow, and change. The important thing is to love everyone you meet. "Bear one another's burdens" (Gal 6:2). "Do good to everyone, especially to the household of faith" (Gal 6:10). That way your words will be sweet, which will be a good thing, just in case you have to eat them!

If I Knew You Were Coming, I'd Have Baked a Cake

WE ARE TOLD IN JOHN 11:5, "Now Jesus loved Martha and her sister and Lazarus" (NIV). Picture this.

Jesus hangs out in Bethany with all His guys at the home of Martha. It must have been a pretty cool house to put up a minimum of sixteen people, probably more. In the theater of my mind, I see Martha pleasantly puttering around in her kitchen in the early morning when Jesus wakes up and comes downstairs.

"How did you sleep? Can I interest you in an egg? Maybe a little toast?" she asks.

I picture Jesus rubbing the sleep out of His eyes with His knuckles, like any other guy. "First, I have to use the bathroom."

And yet, He's not like any other guy.

Later, when their brother, Lazarus, gets super sick, Martha and Mary call for Jesus. Lazarus gets sicker and dies.

Martha loves Jesus. She sends for Him, and He eventually comes, but seemingly too late.

She says, "Lord, if you had been here my brother would not have died" (John 11:21 NIV). Mary has the identical response. What an interesting learning curve: fear, unmet expectation, frustration, grief, bewilderment, astonishment, and joy. It seemed like He was too late, but Jesus had other plans, plans that weren't in Martha's framework of possibilities. Resurrection.

These girls needed to continually allow their mindsets, ideas, and frames of reference to be challenged and informed by Jesus. So difficult!

Shortly after that, Jesus chose to submit to crucifixion to fulfill God's plan of redemption, to fulfill the Law, and it could not have been more confusing for these girls. Jesus was like any other house guest in some ways, and yet He was not like anyone else. He put off His deity, was born, lived, and was put to death to atone for my sin and glorify the Father. He rose from the dead, ascended into heaven, and now He intercedes for me.

John 12:25-26 says, "Whoever loves his life loses it, and whoever hates his life in this world will keep it for eternity. If anyone serves me, he must follow me and where I am, there my servant will be also. If anyone serves me, the Father will honor him."

This is all causing me personal friction because secretly I pride myself on my survival skills: (1) I don't suffer fools lightly. (2) I can easily spot a con artist. (3) I don't tolerate abuse, and I don't let people take advantage of me. (4) I'm not gullible.

Lately, however, I've been sensing that the Lord is asking me to dial down my defense mechanisms. Maybe it isn't my responsibility to protect God's honor or my own. Perhaps God isn't concerned with making sure that idiots don't mess up my stuff. Mostly though, I'm being asked to lay down my desire to understand exactly what is happening and my need to be in control of it. I'm being asked to invest my affection in some tough customers who may not give me a return on my investment. This is risky business.

Martha surely didn't have the luxury of understanding or controlling the events at her own house. She had to trust that Jesus and the events associated with Him were on His own time schedule. She was not in charge.

What if she knew that some of Jesus' disciples were disloyal, like Judas? Did Peter mess up her house with his impulsivity, or invite more people to dinner? Just some things I wonder about.

Martha could only say *yes* or *no* to hosting Jesus, just like us. She said *yes,* and as a result, she was able to give provision and protection to the Lord of glory. She had to learn to keep an open mind and to trust Him. This resulted in a very precious friendship with Jesus Himself. So, I'm inspired because that's all I really want anyway. How about you?

Cake and Candles

OUR LOCAL TV WEATHER GUY is cheerful, articulate, and prone to wax eloquent about meteorology. He seems excited to announce that this has been the coldest February in recorded history, a little too chipper if you ask me. With three days left in the month, it kind of feels like living on the moon. Just going outside is tricky because it requires layers of special clothes, boots, and gloves—like an astronaut on a moonwalk after leaving the lunar module. It makes you do some deep freezer diving before you zip out for milk and bread. "Here kids! We don't need bread. I found hot dog buns in the freezer."

All I can tell you is that winter and the prolonged darkness get fatiguing. Personally, I fight the urge to be grumpy, hungry, or whiney continually. The Instagram pictures of people's recent spiritual burden for Caribbean and Central American people groups aren't helping either.

One wonders how to cope. Pasta, Romano cheese, artichokes,

and grilled chicken will do for me. To that recipe, I add friends, hungry friends, bearing warm garlic bread and a good playlist. After they leave, I resort to hot baths, magazines, and candles—all at the same time.

Funny, isn't it, that only two months ago I was enjoying chestnuts roasting on an open fire and jingling sleigh bells and all that Christmassy jazz? Now, it's just dark and cold and frosted in white. Kind of like the first Christmas, I guess, except without the white.

There was such darkness back in those days, two thousand years ago, a darkness hard to even imagine. Israel was occupied by the hostile armies of the Roman Empire. The merciless soldiers were everywhere, and the Jews were afraid and miserable. Oil lamps in houses flaming on cold winter nights didn't do much to penetrate the dark despair brought on by hopelessness.

Then, when it seemed like the night would never end, God in heaven enacted His plan, sending the Daystar as the light of men. Jesus left His throne in heaven, made His way to earth, and permanently took care of our sins.

According to a physician named Luke, the angel Gabriel came to a teenage girl named Mary and told her that she was going to become pregnant by the Holy Spirit, have a son, and name him Jesus. It took her fiancé, Joseph, an angelic visit to be convinced that her story was true—one angel to confirm another angel's story. That's kind of an amazing story, but that's what happened.

As it turned out, Mary and Joseph were in Bethlehem getting their taxes done when the baby arrived. He had to be born in a barn because there were no rooms left in the city. More angels got involved and announced the baby's birth to shepherds who were guarding sheep. Important men from the Middle East came with gifts for the baby. It was all pretty incredible. But it had to be for a holy God to relate to sinners like you and me. God had to do the impossible; He had to send His Son, born of a virgin, to live and then die on the cross to fulfill the Law. Jesus lived a sinless life, was nailed to a cross, and was buried to atone for our sins, and God, by His power, raised Him from the dead. Jesus made a way for us to be identified with Him in His death and, therefore, be forgiven.

The Bible says we should believe in our hearts and then go tell others in order to receive salvation. God pours all His favor on us because we are identified with His Beloved Son. Jesus comes into our hearts and makes us new. And that's just the beginning! Then, He encourages us to let His light shine through our lives, kind of like birthday candles. Now, that helps me to more than cope with this winter; it fills me with hope.

Part 4:
Pastry Chef

Have Some Cake!

WHINING IS GOING AROUND THESE days like the flu! I'm complaining because up here in western New York we have a season called *pastel ski jacket*, which means the calendar says spring, but snow is still falling. I feel like I haven't been warm since Labor Day.

Today, I was reading in 1 Kings 19, and it sounds like whining is not a new sport.

First Kings 19:1-8 tells us Elijah just had a major victory over the bad guys (prophets of Baal), and Jezebel was hopping mad because those bad guys were her favorites. She breathed out murderous threats against Elijah, and he ran. Somehow, the confidence he was supposed to hang on to after his major victory had leaked out. He was tired and upset.

God was not put off by his little tantrum. Elijah told God he wished he were dead. God's response was so maternal. I love it. First, Elijah needed a nap under a shady tree. After a bit, an angel woke him and offered him some cake and water. Not bad. Then, he went for a second nap, woke up, and had more cake. What good advice for exhausted people! Moms know that naps and snacks work wonders!

It goes on to say in 1 Kings 19:9-18, Elijah was hiking up on Mt. Horeb, but he was still pretty cranky. He eventually finds himself a cave on the side of the mountain where he rests again. The Lord comes to Elijah, and he asks him, "What are you doing here, Elijah?" Can you imagine? Elijah is a little huffy with God. He said something like this: "You know, I have been very committed to Your honor, Lord. The people have been rotten, and now they're trying to kill me! I'm the only decent guy left around here."

I love what God did next. God said, "Let Me show you a few things."

So, God showed Elijah a windstorm, an earthquake, and a fire. Pretty scary.

Then, God started to whisper. Elijah came to the opening of the cave to have a better listen. God goes on to explain how He is going to send someone to help Elijah.

You see, God didn't yell at him. He showed Elijah His power and His glory. Then, God told Elijah to go find Elisha, who ended up assisting him. God also informed Elijah, "Oh, by the way, I have seven thousand other prophets who have not sold out to Baal. You're not alone." God doesn't condemn Elijah. He comforts the prophet, and then He enlightens him.

Psalm 23 says, "He leads me beside still waters. He restoreth my soul" (KJV). God is merciful, not harsh. He shows Elijah His power, and then He sends Elijah some help. He's sort of like a mother who makes her child a sandwich, gives him a nap, and then says, "I'll handle it. Let me help you."

That's how God is. Even though I need to learn how to maintain a joyful attitude, God is not offended by my whining. He wants to show you and me how glorious He is so that we will be encouraged.

Self-pity saps your strength, makes you tired, and discouraged, and extra vulnerable to sin. God wants to show you how wonderful He is so that you will be filled with courage and hope. So, go ahead and have some cake!

Getting Creamed

THOSE OF US FROM BUFFALO tend to be two types of people. There are those who realize that the winter weather can be treacherous to drive in and, therefore, find it wiser to stay in the safety of their homes during snowstorms. And, then, there are fools who consider the meteorologists and TV weather people to be alarmists who use their fancy virtual maps and ill-fitting suits to intimidate and bully us poor stir-crazy souls into staying home. I guess you know now what type I am.

Anyway, the talking weather heads keep making reference to an "Arctic Vortex." I'm pretty sure they stole that phrase from a sub-par movie starring Dennis Quaid back in the nineties about an apocalyptic freeze occurring in Manhattan. How corny.

So earlier this week, I needed to take my sweet, eighty-something mom back home to Buffalo from my house. It's an hour away. And, of course, my husband told me that I should take mom home on Sunday evening before the snowstorm hits, but I wasn't feeling particularly road-trippy on Sunday. I waited until Monday.

Having finished work early that afternoon, I figured I had plenty of time to take Mom to Buffalo and then return home before it got dark. I thought, *How bad could the snow be in daylight?* Then, I loaded up "Grandma," as she's known to my kids, and her rolly bag at about 2:30. The sun was out. I knew I had plenty of time.

The way there was pretty uneventful, but it had started to snow. Grandma said that the ride home might be better on the two-lane road back to my house rather than the four-lane toll road. After dropping her at the back door of her apartment building, I hightailed it out of there.

The wind began to pick up, and I could feel it tug at my car as I drove east. The snow that had fallen began to blow across the roads, causing squalling and momentary whiteouts, but I wasn't too concerned. I had Alicia Keys and Adele on the radio, and I felt empowered and brave!

My mother lives in upscale suburb complete with antique stores, art galleries, and Talbots Normally I scan the store fronts as I drive past. This time, instead, I had to keep my eyes glued on the Lexus in front me.

I had a little trepidation at that point, but mostly the challenge invigorated me. It wasn't until I was leaving civilization and the road became two lanes and rural that the snow came down heavier and the wind became stronger.

I switched the pop radio station to a Christian radio station. I needed to build my faith at that point. I was getting scared. I had the defrost and the temperature set on high, but I don't think that was why I was sweating. When I looked through my car windows, it looked like I had been immersed in milk. I couldn't see the road or its edges. All I could see was white. Not good. Thankfully, a guy in a big electrical truck, complete with the bucket thing on top, pulled out in front of me. I focused on his happy, little, red lights for a long time. When he finally pulled into his own driveway, I was sad but grateful, like a hitchhiker. I crawled into Batavia which looked like Bedford Falls in *It's a Wonderful Life*. I was relieved.

As I headed out of Batavia on the two-lane road, it got bad. I turned off the radio and began to pray in earnest. I couldn't pull over or bail out to a motel because in the morning I had a doctor's appointment for my daughter. It had taken more than eight months to get in to see this specialist. I had to get home.

I crawled along searching for the white line at the right-hand side of the road. My biggest fear was driving into a ditch or into an oncoming vehicle and getting creamed.

I crept along the mostly abandoned roads until I came to the little village right before mine. "Just a few more miles," I reassured myself. My own driveway looked fabulous to me. My husband was not impressed. He had been right.

The ride ended up taking me more than twice the amount of time that it should have under normal weather conditions. I had shooting pains in my neck and back from the stress, and I was wet with perspiration, but I was safe.

I guess all those foreboding weather people had been right. Maybe it isn't always media-hype when they say, "Stay in!" Why is it that some people heed warnings and others don't?

Lord, help me to be wiser in the future, and thank You for the company on Route 33.

Cake on the Table

T HE CITY OF BUFFALO IS a curious place. It has the strange mix of former glory, palpable despair, and the nagging suspicion that great days are just ahead.

The people who lived in my old neighborhood were the first generation to be born in the United States, having parents who were born in Italy, Poland, or Greece, or the first generation to climb out of poverty. No one ever won tickets to this neighborhood. God forbid you lost your school shoes; you only had one pair.

I moved an hour down the road to another city in upstate New York when I was eighteen. I didn't even have a driver's license. I was so intimately acquainted with the Greyhound station that, once, the ticket window guy asked me, "What happened to your red coat? I liked that coat." *Geez.*

I thought that I could breathe easier in that nearby city. It had more oxygen. So, I stayed.

I attended several little Christian colleges where I added

Pentecostal and Free Methodist layers to my spiritual self. The people at these schools were incredibly kind to me. Maybe they sensed that I was trying to learn certain dance steps that I'd never been taught. Being the first person in your family to graduate from college is a certain form of pioneering. I'm sure of it.

Fast-forward a few years. Why is it that some of us spend our lives fighting the feeling that we're caged in? I live in an average suburban neighborhood. My neighbors neither have maids nor housekeepers, neither do they work in these positions. We wash our own cars and mow our own lawns, with some pride that we even have lawns.

I'm at this place where I'd rather experience something awe-inspiringly beautiful than have cool housewares. I don't know why I'm like this, but I fight feeling caged in.

I'm reminded of a beautiful littler terrier I owned. Her name was Stella. She was tan and silver with a black undercoat that made her look like she needed a root touch-up. I named her after a hairdresser I used to know.

Now, Stella had this terrible habit. She loved to slip out and run around the neighborhood. She loved to escape the safety of my house, and she loved to chase cars. So, on September 11, while I was watching horrible smoking buildings on my television, Stella got out as my preschooler was coming in from the backyard.

The next thing I know, there were two twelve-year-old boys at my door saying, "We think your dog just got hit by that school bus."

You want to know the truth? I'm an escapist, too. I longingly imagine myself in exotic places. I want more excitement. I want more action. I'm more jealous of people's trips than of their stuff. I don't want to stay where I belong. I want to chase buses.

Lord, help me not to long to escape the day that I live in. Help me not to pine for other places or circumstances. Help me to be satisfied with the bread at my table (or preferably cake). Help me to not chase buses. Help me to remember that "godliness with contentment is great gain."

"Cake by the Ocean"

I GUESS I'M NOT THE ONLY one who feels trapped, stifled, or whatever else one may call it. (Cue the Jimmy Buffet music and roll the tropical beach footage, panning past a straw hut and chaise lounge chair to the crashing surf.) These days, I read travel magazines with relish and abandon. I subscribe to a few and glance at others every time I'm near a newsstand.

Conde Nast is my candy. *Travel and Leisure* are my personal friends. These magazines always lure me with headlines like, "Best Secret Beaches" and "Exotic Escapes."

This year these are calling me louder than ever! The tropical sites have more than a gentle tug on my mind. But because I'm in prayer, I'm asking God, "What is my problem?"

You know what the Holy Spirit said?

He said, "You want beautiful light. You want gentle warmth. You want a fragrant breeze. You want clear water. Let Me be those needs to you. I can do that. Let Me captivate you with the beauty of the light of My face. Let Me comfort you with the warmth of My presence. Let Me invigorate you with the fragrance of My love. Let Me refresh you with the washing of My Word. You just need more of Me."

No lie. He said it. I heard it last Wednesday while I was driving to work at seven in the morning, in the dark.

"Is that you, God?"

"Yep."

The psalmist said, "Let the light of your face shine on us" (Ps 4:6 NIV). I want to be captivated by the light of His face. I want to be in His face.

The Lord longs to show us how He feels about us, what promises He wants to fulfill in our lives. He wants to tell us about our inheritance as the King's much loved daughters. He wants to hear the full range of our emotions. He can handle our emotional honesty.

Oftentimes, we are brutally honest about how we feel to people but not to God. But He wants us to come to Him, to spend time in His face so that He can speak to us.

Many people in the Bible sought "God's face" during trials, especially David the psalmist and even the Lord Jesus Himself. What stops us from spending time, "seeking His face?"

Perhaps it's hard for us to believe that God Himself really desires to speak to us.

Sometimes, we can fall into the trap of thinking, "Well, I trusted God before, and it didn't work."

You might think He's mad at you. Or maybe you're mad at Him?

It's impossible for God to be disillusioned with you. He never had a false illusion about you in the first place.

Disappointment can mess us up. I believe that it's possible to have experienced disappointment with God that keeps us from enjoying His presence. We may have misinterpreted what actually happened. God may have lovingly spared us from the thing we wanted. Thankfully, the path that we've taken has led us to God Himself.

So, what do we do?

We release the care of wondering why or assigning blame. Though tempted to avert our gaze or pout, we determine to trust that the Lord is good and choose to start fresh—to actually believe Him! Then, we will more clearly see His face.

Furthermore, we allow God to comfort us. Psalm 16:11 says, "You have let me experience the joys of life and the exquisite pleasures of your own eternal presence" (TLB). The Message says, "Now you've got my feet on the life path, all radiant from the shining of your face. Ever since you took my hand, I'm on the right way." And the English Standard says, "You make known to me the path of life; in your presence there is fullness of joy; at your right hand are pleasures forevermore."

The Lord sounds like a travel brochure! He's not upset for my desires for beauty and refreshment. His presence can make all the difference in all the world!

A Foolproof Recipe

N O DOUBT, YOU'VE HEARD THE phrase, "Look before you leap." Well, that works okay with swimming holes and business deals, but a leap of faith is slightly different.

I secretly think that, before you can take a leap of faith, you need to believe that there's something out there that's worth leaping for. There needs to not only be a certain discontentment with your current level of peace, satisfaction, or fulfillment, but there also must be a bubble of hope. I think that, when you hear about a new way of doing things, you should have enough eager expectation that it could be what you've been looking for all along.

Hope springs up when you sense the Holy Spirit drawing you to take the leap to commit your heart to Jesus. After that, you may be at a place where you want more power for godly living, more joy, better health—where you want more cake. All of this is available to us by the power of the Holy Spirit.

The Holy Spirit wants to fill you so full that it spills over into joy and thanksgiving for you and then splashes onto others as a refreshing blessing. That hope does not disappoint you because it comes from God. He puts the longing in your soul, gives you the grace to believe, and then He Himself satisfies that longing.

Believing in the first place, then, is kind of like falling in love. It's a beautiful, exciting time when every detail of the story of how you came to faith is important. "You confess with your mouth the Lord Jesus and believe in your heart," as Romans 10:9 says (NKJV). It sort of sounds like a wedding—like the beginning of something sweet where two lives thus joined partake of cake before embarking on the rest of their journey. From here on out, the adventure unfolds.

But the truth is, we're living in families, local churches, and communities where there is a disconnect between our spiritual lives and seeing the miraculous in thriving at work, enjoying married life, lovingly raising and educating kids, and helping others do the same. So, the question remains: How can we know God better, get to enjoy the Companion of our souls, understand what He says, and please Him?

If you don't already have lots of seasoned people in your life who explain and model the supernatural life—how to live in the tension of believing for what God promised while still having your feet firmly planted in regular life—don't fret. According to Acts 2:42, God's plan for each of us is to devote ourselves to "the apostles' teaching and the fellowship, to the breaking of bread and the prayers." What happened when the early church did this?

> Awe came upon every soul, and many wonders and signs were being done through the apostles. And all who believed were together and had all things in common. And they were selling their possessions and belongings and distributing the proceeds to all, as

any had need. And day by day, attending the temple together and breaking bread in their homes, they received their food with glad and generous hearts, praising God and having favor with all the people. And the Lord added to their number day by day those who were being saved. (Acts 2:43–47)

Here is the simplest recipe for spiritual health that I've ever found. It amounts to this: Study the Bible with mature people, go to church, eat together in each other's homes, share your money and your stuff with those in need, and pray. This is the first prescription for healthy spiritual growth, and even though it can take many different forms, I think this is still a foolproof recipe.

Hungry?

WHEN PEOPLE WANT YOU TO dial down your passion and relax, they say things like, "Leave well enough alone," or, "Nothing's perfect." In Scripture, however, we see time after time that God responds to those who relentlessly hunger for more and want to take it up a notch. Such characters took risks, and sometimes it looked like they upset the people in charge. I've been thinking lately about one Bible character in particular—Rahab, the girl who owned a Traveler's Inn in Jericho with a clean, comfortable bed and the option for sex.

After Moses led the people out of Egypt, Joshua was chosen to lead them into the Promised Land. Joshua sent out two spies to scope out Jericho to see how best to conquer it while the rest of the people waited on the other side of the Jordan. When the two spies went into the city, they immediately went to Rahab's house.

Scholars say that the only way she could have owned an upscale house in the city wall, with great views, was that she was in semi-retirement. They say that she had probably been a concubine to an important city official at one time. The home was a severance package, a golden parachute. Remember, this was before Botox.

Rahab was probably shrewd, savvy, and a little tired; she was neither young nor old. One thing we can count on, she was insightful, perceptive, and ready for change.

Here's the thing: When she saw the spies, men who were strangers, she immediately gave them her confidence and her resources. She hid them from the city officials, she helped them escape, and she even lied for them. Is it possible that in her heart she had been longing for more for a long time? Perhaps there was a desperation in her heart for change that had been brewing for quite a while. Could she have been fed up with the status quo, big house, or no big house.

I think she had been crying out for more. Her heart said, *This can't be it, God. There must be more.*

So, when she saw the spies, she knew. *This is it. These guys and their awe-inspiring God have come to change everything.* And they did.

The children of Israel marched around the city walls, and the city walls fell. The lives of Rahab and her family were spared.

Rahab lost her house and business, her community, everything. One thing remained, however, for Rahab out of all that devastation. I believe she experienced renovation of her heart. She wanted more, and God answered the cry of her heart.

I believe her life changed because she asked God for more, and God answered her prayer. She embraced her new-found, miracle-working God and His people.

Here's another thing: I can take comfort in knowing that God sees my desire for more of Him. God will also engineer supernatural opportunities to those who are expectantly looking for more of

Him. I can also be assured there are other hearts that God has prepared to hear the gospel from people like me. He knows how to make people spiritually hungry. He is working all around us all the time.

It's possible that, when you open your mouth to make reference to what God has done and is doing in your life, there will be people listening who are eagerly waiting for that very important message, like their life depends on it. They are ready to respond because they have been waiting, wishing, and praying for some game-changing news, like the gospel. When they hear it from you, they'll respond immediately, just as Rahab did.

No Cake Walk

Lately, I've thought a lot about sin and the culpability of those with mental illness. I mean, can I hold the individuals in my life who have been diagnosed with a disorder accountable for wrongdoing? At what point are they held accountable for ... well ... sin? I've decided that this is a sticky topic, but it's one that I've got to wrestle with at least a little bit.

My own brother has always been a horse of a different color. He was diagnosed with bipolar disorder. It's been hard to know how to hold him accountable to what he knows is true and right, especially as it pertains to my mother.

I've wondered what her role is in his life, a man in his sixties, seeing she is in her eighties. Should she be his caregiver? I know that my mom sometimes gets weary in the process of supporting him. After all, he is a grown man, and she is a senior citizen. Sometimes, he's stable. Sometimes, he's not.

Here's one for consideration: How does it look to believe in

God for miracles for those we love who live with the not-so-nice reality of mental illness—and still have patient faith?

My own daughter was recently diagnosed with "PDD-NOS," which stands for *Pervasive Developmental Disorder: not otherwise specified.* This is a disorder also known as autism. I find myself wading through sheaves of paper that pertain to the special accommodation that must be made for my little girl and her education. Anyone who has had to persevere over any length of time in matters that aren't easily resolved knows that these long processes can be discouraging.

Ultimately, I convinced the school district that my daughter needed to be in a smaller setting than the public middle school. People told me they would never agree to that. So now, after six months of meetings and evaluations and paperwork, the committee agrees with me. I wasn't expecting to be weepy at this point. I should be elated. Right?

Reality is not pretty. The reality is, my little girl is so out of sync that she needs a specific program not offered in my home school district. I feel like I'm about to head into the *Twilight Zone.* I think I'm afraid of the unknown. Dread is sapping my strength. Maybe though, it will be better. People will be better equipped to work with her. It might be way smoother. I mean, if I needed wheelchair ramps attached to my house, I wouldn't say, "They're messing up the curb appeal." No, I'd be grateful.

My son told me the reason that I'm blue is because I'm having to concede my original expectation of band concerts, chorus concerts, school musicals, school sports teams, etc. My challenge is to believe that God is still authoring a great story even if it's one that I can't imagine. I have no framework for what it might be. I know what normal looks like, but I've seen bad, too. I think I'm being forced to anticipate something different but good. Redefining success, that's what's being asked of me.

My kid will get what she needs and will not be damaged in the process. That's my new definition of success.

In the meantime, I went to visit the program that the school district recommended for my daughter only to find out that it's full for next year. *Are you kidding me?* I went through six months of negotiations on her behalf only to find out that it recently filled up. I'm going home to have a combination intercession-tantrum.

They never really tell you how. I mean, they tell what to do concerning the one you love. They tell you about the medicine, about the procedure, or about the process. No one tells you how you will cope, or how you will get through it. Am I allowed to blame someone? The chasm between what I was hoping for and what I got, how do I span that? My primary enemy is my expectation, which always gets me in trouble.

Here's what I've come up with: Jesus is enthroned. His finished work on Calvary has purchased all I need, including rest. According to Hebrews, Jesus entered into every human detail of daily life. He's seen it all. Autism doesn't scare Him. It isn't too intense for Him. He's not embarrassed to be seen with me or my inappropriate daughter. He's not frustrated by me or her. Jesus is my example, and He can provide rest for my soul.

The thing with mental illness is, it's exhausting. It's hard work. I've decided that it's okay to need supernatural peace after dealing with her emotional episodes.

Peace is different than escape. Peace means that the Holy Spirit is guiding me to a Sabbath rest that involves trusting Him for what I cannot understand or see—trusting Him for and with the future. This rest, this peace comes by choosing to believe. It comes by faith. Ironically, this peace involves work. The work is putting on faith when it slips off. Sometimes, it involves repenting from entertaining fear. At other times, it involves dismantling the room I made for fear.

My Savior took on flesh and blood. He saw tired, discouraging moments. I figure I'm about the same age His mom was when He finished His work here on earth. I wonder if He gave her gray hair?

God is not ashamed of my humanity. He is not unfamiliar with disappointment and pain. Hebrews says that Jesus holds everything together by His powerful Word. Sometimes, it's me He must hold together, especially when I'm losing it. It's He who sustains me.

I am being asked to give nurture, affection, instruction, protection, and correction to a tough customer. By definition, people with autism are self-focused. I'm asking God to dispatch some of those angels that are referred to in Hebrews 1. I need some of those ministering spirits to assist me in what I'm called to do. I'm asking them to protect us, to make provisions for us, to make our path smooth. That's what I'm asking God. Believe me, it's no cake walk.

I'm not going to fixate on what's not perfect. I'm going to take some of the peace and rest that was purchased for me. If someone bought food for me, I would eat it. That's how I'm going to consider the provision of God. He bought it; I ought to receive it. I'm not going to lose my own sanity trying to find some for her. I've seen that. Not good.

Hebrews 5:2 says, "He can deal gently with the ignorant and misguided" (NASB). Well, then, so can I. At least that's the goal.

Cake for the Soul

A COUPLE DAYS AGO, MY MOTHER called me to tell me that my older brother, Jimmy, has cancer of the esophagus. He's sixty. He's been a lifelong smoker, he's bipolar, and he's a little homeless; that is to say, he rents a room from a guy in the city during the week and then sleeps on my mother's couch on the weekend.

My mother and brother go to church together. He keeps his church clothes at her apartment. He likes to wear pinstriped suits with black shirts and a tie. He wears his hair gelled back. He's got a pretty distinctive style. When he was younger, he was in and out of trouble a lot. He was the drummer in the school band from the time he was nine until he was about sixteen. He was ADHD before doctors diagnosed it, and he probably could have used meds. My parents argued about him constantly, and my dad eventually left. As his younger sister, it was difficult to be associated with him. Teachers and administrators would ask me if I was his sister, and then they'd say things like, "Well, in that case, I'll be keeping an eye on you."

Throughout Jimmy's twenties and thirties, he was in and out of jail, in and out of the military, and in and out of a place to live. He attended both the colleges that I attended after I had graduated and subsequently took advantage of my friends. Once he told some guys that, if they worked for him, he would pay them when the roofing job was done. They called me and told me that he owed them money. I said, "Join the club."

One time, he left a disabled truck on the property where he was staying. They called me repeatedly to see if I could remove the truck. It stayed there until the homeowner (my friend) finally had it towed.

The fact is, Jimmy scared my friends. Sometimes, he slept in Salvation Army collection bins full of clothes. Having the police at our kitchen door was not that unusual. But my Karl is a rock solid guy who has always protected me from the family craziness

Fast forward the film thirty years, and here I am, being asked to put aside my childish frame of reference. It's time to stop thinking of Jimmy as one, non-stop pain in my neck. It's time to get over my resentment for not being able to control his behavior. As a matter of fact, he's been fairly subdued for about ten years now.

The other ongoing point of contention between us is that he continually depletes our mom of her resources, emotionally, physically and financially. I hate that. She's a widow who lives in subsidized housing herself!

At this point, I think that I can find the grace to support my mom as she supports him. That's the least I can do. After all, Jesus said:

> "For I was hungry and you gave me food, I was thirsty and you gave me drink, I was a stranger and you welcomed me, I was naked and you clothed me, I was sick and you visited me, I was in prison and you came

to me." Then the righteous will answer him, saying, "Lord, when did we see you hungry and feed you, or thirsty and give you drink? And when did we see you a stranger and welcome you, or naked and clothe you? And when did we see you sick or in prison and visit you?" And the King will answer them, "Truly, I say to you, as you did it to one of the least of these my brothers, you did it to me." (Matt 25:35–40)

Cake Topping, Show Stopping

JUST WHEN I THOUGHT I'D heard everything, this happened.

I called my eighty-six-year-old mother three days in a row. No answer. So, I panicked a little and called Jimmy. Here was the conversation, more or less.

Me: "Have you seen Mom?"

Jimmy: "Yeah, she's driving ladies in her building to the grocery store."

Me: "Good. I was nervous about her. Where are you now?"

Jimmy: "I'm just coming out of the VA hospital. They say I'm cancer free. They can't find the lesions that they had previously seen. Praise God!"

Me: "Wow! That's awesome!"

Jimmy: "Yeah, they just lasered off layers of tissue in there just to be on the safe side."

Me: "Incredible!" I was totally amazed. Funny, isn't it, how we're shocked when God comes through and fulfills our petitions?! I was especially happy that my mother was not going to be burdened with pulverizing his food anymore. That was daunting. But wait! It got better.

My brother says to me, "How can I pray for you?"

Wait, what? My mind can't believe my ears. My brother has never said that to me in my entire life. I would have told you that he's genetically self-absorbed. This has me crying.

Me: "Well, I'm struggling with...." I go on to tell him some stuff.

Jimmy: "Well, why don't I pray for you right now?" And he does!

That was a first. My brother prayed powerfully for me in a way that I've never heard him pray. I was a weepy mess because, even though I had received encouragement from God before, it never came from my older brother. I would have to say that he is changing. God is healing his mind, his soul, and his body, and while God healing people's bodies is not all that unusual to me, people developing empathy seems really miraculous!

Holiday Food

WHENEVER I READ ABOUT NEHEMIAH, I'm always amazed at his ability to simultaneously feel the heart of God, see what needs to be done, kindle vision in other people, delegate tasks, operate in some crazy supernatural authority, cooperate with Ezra, shepherd the people's souls, fend off bad local officials, finish the task, and celebrate! I think the nature of his genius was not only his particular mix of giftedness, but, more importantly, it was his perspective. He was a multi-faceted guy who knew how and when to change his hat. No small feat.

People throughout history are always eager to tell you why their particular historical crossroads are more challenging than ever before, but I think what it boils down to is perspective. For Nehemiah, after the wall around Jerusalem was finally finished and the Book of the Law was found and read, everyone was tempted to despair because how far short they fell as a people from God's ideal. Nehemiah, once again, had the supernatural perspective. He said, "Go home and prepare a feast, holiday food and drink; and share it with those who don't have anything: This day is holy to God. Don't feel bad. The joy of God is your strength" (MSG).

People never tire of criticizing their political leaders, lamenting the economic climate, revealing some new evil threat to normal life. Friends of mine just sent their fourteen-year-old daughter back to high school after her having a grueling year fighting leukemia, complete with a bone marrow transplant from her sister. Now, she's going back to her sophomore year of high school. The doctors say that she even grew two inches taller over the course of the year. This is cause for rejoicing.

At moments like these, we need to take the time to rejoice and have a party that will replenish our strength. Taking the time to celebrate triumphs and answered prayer is important because it not only builds us back up, but it also encourages those who still need the strength to keep fighting. Testifying builds faith. Why is it so much easier to sound an alarm than to bring a good report?

We are encumbered by all the sorrow around us that is real, by the way, not imagined. At the same time, we need to look for opportunities to be thankful, grateful and joyful along the way, to replenish our strength. Otherwise, we will have no strength to fight when we really need it for the battle

Bruce Wilkinson in his book, *Secrets of the Vine,* said that, when people come through the wilderness, they will need time to recover and heal. We probably would get farther if we knew better the rhythms of working, fighting, celebrating, and resting. That could be the key for going the distance in victory.

God is not most impressed with who can go the longest without rest or recreation. The goal is knowing how to manage the call of God, one task at time, living in the day that we're in, knowing when to rest, when to work hard, when to party, and knowing when to take the time to be alone with the Master to have our own vision refreshed by His peace and His presence.

Some Assembly Required

EXPERIENCING GOD'S PRESENCE, READING HIS Word, fasting for breakthrough, worshiping with fellow believers—these things don't happen on their own. They require participation and even work on our part. It's kind of like food shopping, cooking, baking, decorating, and serving don't happen by passively wishing. You have to roll up your sleeves and get at it!

Richard J. Foster, in his spiritual classic *Celebration of Discipline: The Path to Spiritual Growth*, wrote:

> Disciplines are best exercised in the midst of our normal daily activities. If they are to have any transforming effect, the effects must be found in the ordinary junctures of human life: in our relationships with our husband or wife, our brothers and sisters, friends, coworkers and neighbors. (1)

In other words, disciplines happen in *the Real*. And their

effectiveness in our lives is evident by how we relate to God and others or respond to circumstances. Didn't realize I'd be revealing my spiritual growth when I make lunches, do laundry, or changed the sheets.

If we desire to go beyond the surface in spiritual matters, we must believe that the Holy Spirit is calling us to explore these disciplines with the same rigor and vigor that we would any new exciting field of endeavor. God desires for us to learn about Him and His Kingdom by practicing these specific, practical aspects of spiritual life.

Each of these areas can be learned and practiced in the same way any incremental learning happens. We can be beginners. That's okay.

As important as knowing what the mechanics of growing in the faith are, that doesn't guarantee that the inner quality of your heart is inclined toward the Holy Spirit. We must humbly present ourselves to want to know Him better.

We want to learn to hear His voice. We want to learn what pleases Him. The wonderful, beautiful truth is that the Lord longs to share with us the secrets of His heart. He wants to guide us into abundant life. He desires to teach us to worship in a way that will enable us to enjoy His presence. He wants to show us His face!

We give ourselves to spiritual disciplines in the way that a new bride or groom begins married life—learning to cook, balance a budget, clean the house, do the laundry, buy an appliance, mow the lawn, and answer questions like: How often do we have to see the in-laws? Does my spouse expect me to iron?

Some things we're naturally better at than others. And so it is with various aspects of growing in godliness. We continue doing what we're good at while honing new skills. We learn what we need to do, what we must do, and what we should avoid.

Shopping for Ingredients

F OR ME, EVERYTHING BEGINS WITH God's Word, and God's Word changes everything. We believe that even though the Bible was written by regular people like you and me, the Holy Spirit uses it to show us God's nature. When we read it we become convinced that every word has meaning for our lives today. We begin to understand God's Word has the power to reveal His plan for our lives.

Over the years, the Bible has been my constant companion. It has helped me hear the voice of the Lord when the circumstances of life were not good. For example, the Lord used the Psalms to comfort me at times when I thought I had lost my mind. When friends were not around, or when they misunderstood me, the Holy Spirit spoke tenderly to me through His Word. The things He spoke to my heart became cherished treasure to me like rubies found in a dark pit.

The Lord desires to reveal His heart to you through His Word.

He will demonstrate to you His affection for you in intensely personal ways. If you record what He tells you, you will end up with a treasure chest or a jewelry box full of gifts from your Beloved Prince of Glory.

These encounters will transform you into the woman God always knew you would be—the woman who knows her God, displays strength, and takes action. No one can take these transformational encounters from you. They become part of your testimony, and no one can negate that. You overcome the enemy by the blood of the Lamb and the word of your testimony.

When you commit the printed Word to your memory and to your heart, it becomes an arsenal of prayer power. It protects you from deception. As David said, "I have stored up your word in my heart, that I might not sin against you" (Ps 119:11). It builds your faith. Mostly though for me, the Bible is the voice of my Beloved whispering in my ear, affirming my beauty and worth. That's what God wants for you, too.

When Bible time seems dry, I pretend I'm grocery shopping. I'm collecting good fruit that I will need eventually, ingredients that will come in handy to feed someone else. It's an adventure when the known and trusted stories take on new meaning or application because my life is changing. The old vanilla pudding becomes crème brûlée!

You'll just have to trust me on these matters. Take time in the Word at the beginning of everyday, calibrate your head with God before you do other adventures, and He will take you on an amazing journey. It may not always be easy, but it will be rewarding!

Preheating the Oven

PRAYER IS A REALLY BIG topic! Books have been written, court cases have been fought, and individuals have spent their entire lives pursuing prayer. What exactly is prayer?

I believe prayer is as simple as believing God wants to speak to me *and* hear what I have to say. To pray and pray effectively, then, I need to settle whether God *does* want to hear from me and *does* have something to say me. Once I believe He does, I have preheated the oven and am ready to pray.

We see in Genesis 1:26 that the Godhead said, "Let us make man in our own image" (KJV). God wanted to reproduce Himself. "Let's make them just like Us," is what He was saying.

Then, we see in Genesis 3:8-11 that God was walking through the garden in the cool of the evening. God customarily talked and walked with Adam and Eve at that time of day. Even after they ate of the fruit, God knew, and He went looking for and calling to them.

Later, in Genesis 12 and again in Genesis 15, we see God sought relationship with Abraham. In fact, God called Abraham. He essentially asked him to be His friend. Abe was the landing strip for God to eventually send Jesus. Through Jesus, we could be reconciled to God, restored to right relationship.

As God desired to walk and talk with Adam, Eve, and Abraham, He desires to walk and talk with us.

God is approachable. Jesus made a way for us to directly access the Father. As a result, we can approach the throne of grace with confidence, "that we may receive mercy and find grace to help us in our time of need" (Heb 4:16 NIV).

God wants to hear from us. He is committed to forgiving us and healing us.

God wants to share His plans with you and me about not only our lives, but also about the lives of the people He loves.

While Jesus was alive, He taught His disciples to pray like this:

> Our Father in heaven, hallowed be your name [endearment, worship, confession, and petitions]. Your kingdom come, your will be done, on earth as it is in heaven. (Matt 6:9-13 NIV)

We believe that God wants us to be His agents who pray down the atmosphere of heaven into the earth. There's no sickness in heaven, no strife in heaven, no jealousy in heaven, and no poverty in heaven.

First Thessalonians 5:17 is a nice recipe/pattern for prayer. It tells us to rejoice always, to pray without ceasing, and to give thanks. Then, it tells us not to quench the Holy Spirit.

When we rejoice, we line our hearts up with God's so He can speak to us. This improves our attitude as we see His perspective. We remain joyful and calm to face the day. Personally, I think the Lord loves to leave us rejoicing.

"Now may the God of peace make you holy in every way, and may your whole spirit and soul and body be kept blameless until our Lord Jesus Christ comes again" (1 Thess 5:23 NLT). He who calls you is faithful, and He will do it.

Supporting Layers

HERE'S ONE FOR THE BOOKS. All the research I did concerning the various psychological diagnoses for my daughter led me to an unexpected verdict. Ready? I'm the one with the ADHD!

No matter what the situation is with my daughter, it didn't take long for me to read the list of symptoms and conclude, "Oh my gosh! This fits me perfectly!" I've always had difficulty paying attention. They called me "dreamy" as a kid because I was looking out the window most of the time. The article went on to say that symptoms include: making careless mistakes, having difficulty organizing tasks, and often losing things like keys, glasses, and phones (WebMD).

Incredible! All this time I just thought I was a batty screw-up! It never occurred to me that I had an issue that could be medically diagnosed. I think that, when I was growing up, people were less likely than they are today to take a little girl to the doctor just because she lost her school shoes every morning. My parents had more important issues than the fact that I missed the school bus all the time. (Did I really hitchhike to high school in a dress? Yes, I did.)

As a college student, I was notorious for my inability to manage my time. Merciful instructors routinely gave me extensions on the deadlines for term papers. And, if you can imagine college life being challenging for someone who was bad at life's details, mothering for me has required nothing short of angelic visitation. "Jesus, take the wheel" had been my mantra way before Carrie Underwood sang it.

I've left graduation parties only to be called by friends saying, "Did you forget something?"

"Like what?", I replied.

"You forgot Gracie, your daughter!"

When I reflect on how I've been able to survive without any pharmaceutical support during my adult life, do you know what I've concluded? It's been people who lovingly corrected and instructed me who have enabled me to compensate.

My husband is an engineer. Every system I use to run my household was his idea. Once, when I was trying to figure out how to keep all the appointments and deadlines straight for my elementary school aged son, my husband suggested that I call my friend, Karen. "Call Karen; she has administrative gifting."

I called her. Karen said that I should buy a planner and that I should unpack my son's backpack, record the dates in the planner, and then throw the papers away. Wow! Mind-blown!

I learned how to take care of my babies by watching and listening to my dear friend, Dawn. We became friends when her son, David, was a student in my kindergarten class. So, when I had my first baby, I just did what she told me, grateful for the coaching. She's the baby whisperer!

Here's the thing. Any of our weaknesses can be compensated

for by listening and obeying friends who have strengths in our weak areas. It's called mutual submission, being vulnerable. I listen to you when you lovingly make suggestions that are in my best interest. Now that I have experience in these areas, I no longer have nearly the struggles I once had. Now, I'm qualified to share how I learned "adulting," even if my ADHD required some "special Ed" instruction.

Angel Food

ONE OF THE CHALLENGES OF having school-aged children is transitioning from the school year, with all its schedules and structure, to summer vacation, which involves trying to figure out whether there should be any structure at all. Do people need to wake up before noon? At what point should someone brush her teeth without being told? I mean, summer vacation means all day swimming and all night bonfires, right?

All this gets more complicated because my one daughter is not necessarily socially inclined. Free time can end up being a mix of watching entire seasons of *Duck Dynasty* or *Clone Wars* on Netflix, all while playing on her DS, with breaks happening only when she's hungry. Setting up some structure is met with no small amount of blowback.

Her: "Leave me alone! This is my vacation!"

Me: "I was thinking you might want to wash your face and put on clean clothes."

So, by the Thursday after the 4th of July, it had escalated into some pretty intense conflict. (As a side note, our erratic schedule makes it difficult for me to remember to give her the meds that allow her to have more emotional margins and fewer blow-ups.)

Me: "Did you have Bible time? Brush your teeth? Unload the dishwasher?"

Her: "Leave me alone!"

It wasn't until after she had stormed out yelling and gotten on her bike that I remembered the meds, her ADHD and anxiety meds. I was upset for having lost my patience. When she came back, I apologized, gave her the meds, and suggested that we go to the public library for some summer reading material. "You don't have to get anything if you don't want to. Just come for the ride," I said to her.

She agreed reluctantly; she was still pretty upset.

When we got to the library, the wildest thing happened. Adam, a senior citizen who runs a chess club for kids at the library, pulled up, got out of his car, stretched out his arms, and yelled, "Oh good! You remembered to come to chess club! Lily, we've missed you. Come help me set up the chess boards!"

Lily became a different person. She was animated, sweet, and helpful. Unbelievable. Adam said to me, "Thank you for bringing her. I've ordered pizza, so you don't have to come back for her until six or seven. Come on, Lily, let's go!"

I looked up to the sky and all I can tell you is that at that moment it seemed like God Himself had kissed me on the lips. He's so personal, so caring.

Thank you, God, for understanding my frailty and my forgetfulness and providing for me anyway. Help me to look to you to give me the grace I need, and to not allow intense moments to be confused with wrecked days.

Part 5:
Cake Boss

Moon Pies

WHEN I WAS STILL IN elementary school, two incredible things happened. Neil Armstrong walked on the moon, and my mother took her one giant step for our family-kind. However, hers was right into the local solar system of a small, white-painted Pentecostal church. She was all geared up for her spacewalk, decked out in her tall white boots, fishnet stockings, hot pants, and Gibson Girl helmet, or should I say, wig, with the poufy up-do effect and big bun on the top. All very fancy and definitely other worldly.

Prior to my mother's entrance into the Final Frontier, the modest suburban neighborhood we lived in made her feel secure. It gave her a sense of belonging. She liked the little houses on tiny lots with sidewalks, streetlights, and chain-linked fences delineating each backyard. The footprint of every house in the neighborhood was exactly the same. I never had to ask my neighbors where their bathroom was; of course, it was to the right of the kitchen.

The three-bedroom ranches with attached one-car garages had

been built as residences for Korean War vets coming home in the late 1950s. The modest dwellings brimming with kids, back in those days, provided a room for the boys and a room for the girls with two sets of bunks in both rooms. If the oldest kid was lucky, he got to customize the basement with black lights, posters, and a mattress atop a pool table. So cool, just saying. I knew people who liked the whole vibe of those neighborhoods so much that they grew up, married, and settled fairly close, but not me.

It might have seemed idyllic if your family was stable and your neighbors friendly, you know, tree-lined streets and all that. If there was arguing, fighting between parents and kids, with an occasional chase-your-son-around-the-outside-of-the-house scene, it was a little difficult to act like nothing was wrong or at least different. If your dad came home drunk and decided to sleep it off in the front seat of his pickup truck, which was parked on the tiny front lawn, walking around that truck with neighboring teens to the bus stop the next morning might be a little tricky to explain or ignore.

The neighborhood seemed like a large, poorly supervised dormitory. You could always hear yelling from the house next door. It was like the whole zip code lacked a vision or a dream to do anything more than get a job at dad's production plant or some uncle's plumber's union.

Unlike the architectural uniformity of my neighborhood, my high school was a completely disheveled anarchy. It was the advent of drugs in high schools. Cigarette smoking was facilitated. The legal age for drinking alcohol was eighteen for a brief season back then. People even kept booze in their lockers. I guess the thinking was, if you can send a kid off to Vietnam after his senior high school trip, then he ought to be old enough to drink beer. The Vietnam War, racial strife, and Nixon's impeachment proceedings weren't helping with scholastic morale. The whole place made me think of the "Fall of the Roman Empire" from history books. It was out of control.

My coping mechanism was to live for Sundays at the Pentecostal church where my mother had started attending. The building smelled of furniture polish mixed with mildew. We alternately froze in the winter and boiled in the summer. I loved it there, though. The people were good to me. They included me, instructed me, and gave me vision. The love and direction I received from those saints might not have been a big deal to them, but it was a big deal to me.

Looking back, they weren't a very elegant crowd. The fathers were mostly delivery men, post office workers, and insurance men. Most of their wives were stay-at-home mothers who gave themselves home perms on Saturday nights. But the nurture they gave me was provision from God Himself. It made me come back to church on Wednesday nights for Bible study or prayer meeting.

A half dozen teens also attended on Wednesdays. We were a little posse. At school, we weren't class officers, sports stars, or the leads of high school stage productions. The teaching and thinking then pressed us to be separate from the world. So, we formed a clan of our own—kind of hanging together in school and then being around each other on Wednesdays and Sundays. And I will forever remember those Sunday school picnics with the seemingly infinite variations on a macaroni salad (Hellmann's or Miracle Whip?), men at the grill in their Father's Day shirts, and Skippy cups of ice cream from the Sunday school superintendent—all a great feast to me. I lived for those days.

So, when the group consensus on what to do after high school was to head off to a nearby Bible college, I was all like, "Sign me up!" I got myself a little waitressing job, saved my money, and headed off to school. Once there, I transferred all my loyalty and affection to a new group of superheroes, my instructors. I stayed on campus year-round as a summer maintenance staff person.

Here, I learned Synoptic Gospels, table manners, and study skills. I went on a missions "internship." It consisted of driving for six weeks to six different cities throughout Mexico in a pickup truck. This resulted in a life-long love affair with the Mexican people, their language, their food, and their culture. After graduating from that school, another paternal instructor suggested I continue on at another school for my bachelor's degree. So, I did.

By then, my parents had split up and sold the house, so I was slightly homeless. I attended this other school, found work, and stayed year-round in its dorm, where yet again I was adopted by merciful, faith-filled saints. Here, I gained an academic and vocational layer. The reality of ministry being something everyone is called to through vocational service was a giant revelation to me.

My experience through the years taught me that, even when my parents were unable to pay attention to what direction, provision, and instruction I needed, the Body of Christ was an agent of God's loving care for me. Married students included me at their humble tables for tea and toast. They modeled stable, peaceful, normal families. They inspired me.

Eventually, I had a modest table of my own, and I was eager to love the lonely. I sensed God's prompting when I invited families or individuals either to my house or to my church, which has always been my second home.

Although my transition to adulthood was bumpy, I learned that, all along, God was leading me to Himself with the breadcrumb path of His goodness, His mercy, and His provision. I learned that, since God was faithful to slowly teach me the ropes and to show me the inner working of the culture of His Kingdom, I could then help share it with others. In other words, I could become the breadcrumb path that others were for me—the path that led me into an intimate and personal relationship with Jesus Christ where I discovered life in the Spirit.

Granola Bars

Yesterday, I stumbled on a box of old snapshots and journals from college. The quality of the photography could not have been worse. The pictures were blurry, dark, and off-center. This was, after all, before digital photography. I saw pictures of myself that are a little embarrassing, depicting bad haircuts, closed eyes, and ridiculous fashion styles. But you know what? God has been faithful to me. You know what's more amazing? By His grace, I've been faithful to Him. By His leading and His sheltering wing, I've been able to walk in the light of His face without any wholesale, wide-scale, falling down a flight of stairs, walking away from God seasons. It's especially noteworthy because I'm not walking on the well-worn path of the generation in front of me. My mother and I are, more or less, "Forrest Gumping" our way through this life of faith.

I have this image of a jungle-dwelling conquistador hacking his way through the rain forest or the swamp with a machete, skin glistening with sweat and wearing a saturated sweatband. That's how it seems to me when you're the first person in your family to walk in God's Kingdom. It's not impossible; it's just not easy. You must go slowly, and you need to sit down sometimes. Other times, you have to back up and rethink your path. You look at the sun and try to remember what the last guy you asked told you. You get frustrated, and you ask lots of questions. You unpack some stuff and throw it away to lighten your load. Then, you learn how to read the map. You study the map. And you get a radio and learn how to tune it to the right station.

The thing is, the people who come after me, the ones who are being trained by my trial and error, can do life on a halfway decent path. They have learned how to read a map and how to tune a radio. They have learned what not to eat or drink. They can recognize subtle signs of sickness and danger.

When I model faith for my kids, teach them to study God's Word, and help them establish a prayer life, they are better equipped to cover more ground and conquer higher mountains than I ever dreamed. I can cheer them on, refresh them, and be a resource for them. I can not only share my granola bars with them, I can also teach them how bake their own and share that knowledge with others, and that's pretty wonderful.

Need a Twinkie?

Aﬀter the death of Joshua, God used a string of mighty men to lead Israel in victory over their oppressors. The Bible calls them judges. Each one fought on God's behalf to bring peace to His people. Here's the plot: Israel chases idols; God gives her into the hands of tormenting heathen nations, and then a deliverer is eventually sent because God can't stand the sound of His crying baby, Israel. Next, peace is restored. Repeat.

In this instance, the deliverer guy's name is Gideon. He always seemed like a Rockstar among the judges to me. God calls him a "mighty man of valor" even though, when God initially finds him, he's hiding in a wine press threshing grain. Did you ever notice how sometimes God calls a talented, valiant person, and other times, he makes one?

God taught Gideon how to be brave. God was patient with him. I can imagine Gideon asking, "God, can I please have a sign, a miracle, *and* a vision—or two?" Eventually, God uses Gideon to win a dramatic victory over the Midianites.

After the initial battle, Gideon and his three hundred men continue to pursue the bad guys. When they come to the towns in the area, Gideon says, "Give my troops some bread; they are worn out" (Judg 8:5 NIV). You see there were no rest areas on their highways with vending machines full of packages of Twinkies or protein bars. They had to ask the people in the towns they passed through for provision.

The city officials from two towns didn't consider Gideon & Company a very good investment. They said, "Why should we give you bread? We don't see any dead kings yet?" (Judg 8:6 my translation). So, without anything to eat, Gideon and his men went and overcame the enemy kings and their giant army. God ordained it. God did it.

You know what bugs me? The town executives were invited to bless a guy who was obviously God's man. What would possess someone to withhold food from a guy "with the bearing of a prince," who was also hungry? (Judg 8:18). Were they threatened? Preoccupied? Cynical?

Here's the thing: Why is it that sometimes the mature people in the Body of Christ act like it will diminish them to promote the younger brothers and sisters who come to us with great anointing? It won't detract from the blessing on our lives but rather promote it. That's how God works.

Let's make it personal. Who in my life could use a slice of cake? There are those all around me who are obviously commissioned by God, and yet I can't be bothered helping them, those who are exhausted yet pursuing the purposes of God?

I believe there is power in my ability to refresh the weary, but first I must actually see them. I need spiritual eyes to see who God is putting in my path. I don't want anyone to go hungry physically or emotionally while it's within my power to feed them and to cheer them on.

Lord, help me to see what You're doing in the earth and to join You in it, even if my role is one that is less than glamorous, like providing cake.

Cake for Bait

JEREMY AND TRAVIS ARE TWO high school hipsters who are cued up to graduate this June. They are handsome, charming, and savvy. They aren't particularly involved in a "school-district-sponsored" way. Jeremy wants to be a writer. I'm not sure what Travis will be pursuing. They haven't exactly found a niche. They both seem a little bit orphaned and slightly aimless, but they're also insightful, and I suspect they're looking for something more meaningful than high school to pin their hopes on.

I find it interesting that they seem to like befriending me. They think I'm fun, and unless they're just so full of malarkey that I'm completely fooled (totally possible), they want to come and hang out at my house, eat my food, and meet my friends.

So, I'm having a dinner party for them. I'm inviting other teenagers who aren't aimless. I want them to see, hear, and feel the better thing that they seek is Jesus. I just have to figure out how to format the gospel in a way that showcases Jesus' goodness and not mine. I have a feeling that they are open to faith. They just don't know it yet, so I'm praying.

The other people I've invited are creative, passionate, worshippers. They are fragrant, fun, highly motivated types. I am convinced that they are extraordinary individuals.

My job is to create an amazing feast complete with blazing fires, roasted meat, groovy music, and possibly a game. Oh, and I need to make some mind-blowing deserts!

Stay tuned!

So, the hipsters tried to cancel on me. I got home from the grocery store, and there was a message, "Mrs. Hoeflein, Travis and I can't make it tonight. He texted me this morning and said that he can't get out of work. Do you think we could reschedule in a few weeks?"

"Well, at this point, I've made homemade custard, cookies, and whipped cream. I've bought steaks and pork tenderloin. My daughter has shoveled off the back deck and bought Tiki torches," I tell Jeremy.

"Travis and I don't have cars 'cause he hasn't bought one and I recently got into a car accident. But that sounds great! And it's so warm outside today, too! Should we just come at 8:45-ish? He should be showered and ready by that time?"

"Yes. Tell him to come after work."

And that's what happened. They came at 9:00 p.m. The teens from church came at 8:30 p.m. It was a stunning candle-lit dinner party, and they were really pleased and a little amazed. The hipsters from church were perfect hosts; they were animated and engaged. They talked about music and schools and culture. I was sort of a background, catering staff person. Dessert was formal tea and vanilla custard with caramel and whipped cream. My daughter, Grace, had made butter cut outs cookies. We served them with fresh raspberries in a dish. Karl and Grace cooked and facilitated and generally added the grooviness to the evening.

The high school boys helped me with the dishes after the others had left. I invited them to the connect group I have for twenty somethings. They were elated that they had stumbled onto new people and a new place. Eventually, they left, Karl went to bed, and I was too busy thanking God to sleep.

Thanks, God.

Holiday Secrets

I'll let you in on a little secret. The holiday season is upon us, and while I enjoy cooking, baking, gift giving, and decorating, there is a pre-requisite to opening your home that no one likes to talk about—cleaning! Yesterday I took a hard look at the piles of old mail and papers on my counter, stacks of magazines, dirty woodwork, grimy walls, and dust balls under my couches. "You can't decorate here. The Board of Health just condemned your house!" Everything needs a onceover with a power scrubber!

I looked at these book shelves in my family room that were crammed with irrelevant paperback books, moldy texts from graduate work I'd done in a previous life, and a myriad of folders filled with notes written on yellow legal pads! Some stuff needed to be given away, but most of it just needed to be thrown out! I'm generally against book burning, but no one would have missed this stuff. And the windows, you can't even see out of them.

In Jeremiah 1:10 in the Message Bible, it makes reference to "pulling up and tearing down" before you can, "build or plant." In my case, that means I'm going to have to tackle some dust bunnies and my dirty fridge before I can hang lights and garland.

I'll be experiencing the true meaning of Christmas because I'm going to have to pray hard before I even start. You're probably one of those people who does fall cleaning from top to bottom so you don't know what I'm talking about, but on the small chance you're not and you're like me, take heart! This could be cathartic! So, stay tuned.

Right now, I am inspired to clean, but if you don't hear anything, it might mean that I've decided instead to dim the lights and light more candles.

A Cake Server

As I'm reading in Acts about the very first days of the followers of Christ who were subsequently filled with the Holy Spirit, it says, "They devoted themselves to the apostles' teaching and to fellowship, to the breaking of bread and to prayer" (2:42 NIV). I say it this way, "They devoted themselves to listening, teaching, eating bread, and praying." Those activities are the most basic and most vital to maturing in faith. This is a really good thing because I like being taught, eating bread, and praying. I so appreciate the simplicity of this formula.

It goes on to say the people shared all things in common, including food, attended the temple, and visited in each other's homes. And on top of all that, many signs and wonders were done (see Acts 2:42-47).

What makes me happy is knowing that opening homes and eating together are two of the earliest hallmarks of people who were endeavoring to grow up spiritually. It means that the notion of sitting in a solitary place, reflecting, and journaling are not the only facets of heathy Christian life. This is good news. It also means that I'm not the first person to have to hide my mess before my friends come over to eat. I'm not the first to throw all my clutter in a laundry basket, to place a vase of flowers on a table, light a candle, or wipe down the bathroom.

Truthfully, when we open our homes to other people, we reveal part of ourselves that can't be seen from afar off. Housekeeping, cooking, decorating, all tell about your priorities and your personal philosophies. We come together in each other's houses so that we can share more intimate parts of ourselves in more intimate settings.

The word *fellowship* seems to have lost the ability to convey anything important. The word has suffered some bad press, and it may be synonymous with greasy casseroles eaten in mildewed church basements and "fellowship halls."

In contrast, I believe that, when we take the time to slow down at a table and eat together, the Holy Spirit in me can connect with the Holy Spirit in you, and if we are both made in God's image, then possibly each of us can showcase a different facet of His image. We can encourage one another and learn from each other. Nothing is as important as how we connect to God, and that may very well be through the person sitting next to me.

Teething Biscuits

On Monday, February 10, 2014, at 10:40 p.m., Bonny Hoeflein wrote:

> Listen to me, O house of Jacob, all the remnant of the house of Israel, who have been born by me from before your birth, carried from the womb; even to your old age I am he, and to gray hairs I will carry you. I have made and I will bear; I will carry and I will save. (Isa 46:3-4 ESV)

You know, it's not that weird to refer to loving babies. Babies are full of promise and possibility. Pregnancies are exciting!

What will that new son or daughter become? We have so much anticipation!

This verse is especially beautiful because it refers to my being important to God with my gray hair in my old age. It says that God will carry me and save me.

I will not become redundant or age out of His love for me. As far as God is concerned, I don't have a sell-by date. I'm going to continue to be important to Him.

Later, in that same chapter God says, "I have spoken, and I will bring it to pass; I have purposed, and I will do it" (v. 11 ESV). It's kind of electrifying to consider that God is committed to fulfilling His promises over my life. He has the power to accomplish what He has in mind—to transform me—and He's not the least bit upset at me for not learning all of life's lessons before my muscle and skin tone give out. That's particularly fantastic since these days a person is supposed to earn advanced degrees, invent something miraculous, get widely published, find Mister Right, start a family, and win a Nobel prize or a Pulitzer before there are any lines in her face.

The expectation that you will conquer all known realms in your youth and become an expert is not realistic or biblical, for that matter. It's good to know that God is committed to me for the long haul. That means He understands that I can be focused on various areas of my life during different seasons, and He is not frustrated with my maturation rate. He has a plan for accomplishing His will for me.

This is news I can use!

Stability from the Bottom Up

T HESE DAYS, THERE IS A widespread pre-occupation with youth and, more importantly, youth culture. The face used in the magazine ad for anti-aging serum is obviously that of a fifteen-year-old girl. The expectation is that a person be successful and significant long before there is grey in her hair. She can also be disheveled, have dirty hair, and not even own a hairbrush, as long as she is under twenty-one. I'm not even going to argue with that phenomenon. My question is: Even if you did conquer all your mountains and hurdles at an early age, then what? Is there an upside to growing older?

I propose that the greatest part about having lived for a little whilelonger than the latest operating system on your iPhone is that you knowsome tribal knowledge about adult life. I heard Bill Johnson say in a sermon recently, "Gifts are free; maturity is expensive." Hopefully, you know some stuff that can only be learned through having had a personal history with God. Confidence and competence are won through personal experiences, not downloaded as an app.

I've lived through moments where I've thought of the words of Old Testament Job, "For the thing which I greatly fear comes upon me, and that which I am afraid has come upon me" (3:25 AMP). Everything from bad breakups, lost jobs, failing courses in school, infertility, and miscarriages to learning disabilities and lice. You know what? God was there through the beautiful and the ugly. No one can take that away from me.

Second Corinthians 6:16 says, "For we are the temple of the living God" (NIV). Paul says that, collectively, we together make up the temple of the living God. And Peter gets in on the analogy when he says, "You yourselves like living stones are being built up as a spiritual house" (1 Peter 2:5). In the very next verse, Peter refers to Jesus as the Cornerstone.

You know what I think? I think those of us who have been around awhile are like foundational stones at the bottom of big, beautiful cathedrals. If you are the first person in your family history to walk by faith, like me, you are a foundational stone. The young people in your life, whether they are your kids or your friends, stand on your shoulders, modeling your faith. The foundation stones in a cathedral are very important even if they aren't adorned like the spires and the stained-glass windows.

They insure the stability of what is built afterwards. If the foundation is unstable, the whole wall falls down, or at the very least, needs lots of expensive excavating and rebuilding. (I've had some of that!) What constitutes unstable foundation stones in the temple of God?

Pettiness, jealousy, self-pity, self-indulgence, and deceitfulness, to name a few. The more mature members of the family also tend to shape the opinions of others, so if those same people are critical and judgmental, that, too, will be reproduced. On the other hand, if your faith over the long haul makes you create a culture of trust, you will be a credible source of inspiration and guidance. So, there you go; your faithfulness is more vital to promoting faith than you realize. Just keep your chins up, both of them!

Test Kitchens

I JUST GOT OFF THE PHONE with a young woman who is a college senior. Her class in creativity has taken a trip to Chicago for a conference. It's a conference on, of all things, creativity.

The presenters sound like the most amazing mix of authors, actors, film producers, tattoo artists, musicians, Cirque du Soleil organizers, and the list goes on and on. I am tempted to be jealous. It seems like the people I know have similar rootstock; they think creatively in their context. They simply don't have this new, improved soil that is available these days. But wait. What if the people who came before, who had the spirit of the pioneer in seed form, are the very foundation of this new breed of creative?

Maybe those of us who value creativity make space and environments for the new entrepreneur. Perhaps it's like a building or castle that has boring foundational stones, blocks really. Not all that exciting. The foundational stones go before and make a way for more exciting, stained-glass windows, turrets, towers, and flag poles to emerge from the top. We who go first hold things up. We provide stable environments and affirmation so that cool endeavors can emerge from our lives. We are like well equipped kitchens where new chefs and bakers can create new kinds of cake and other delicacies. We are like mature trees that provide sturdy, shady, green places for others to come and build their nests and grow. We stay submitted to the call on our lives, to the local church, and to our communities so that innovation can proceed from our stability, resources and strength.

No Cake Smashing

HOW DO YOU FEEL ABOUT cake-smashing? You know that time at a wedding reception where the bride and groom cut the cake and then feed it to one another?

People tend to be from one school of thought or the other. smashers or non-smashers. Personally, if I applied make-up for an hour on the most important day of my life, I wouldn't want frosting smooshed all over my face, but that's just me. In my mind, it seems demeaning or disrespectful, a little crass. It's a good thing my husband probably already knew that.

Revelation 21:9 makes reference to the Body of Christ (meaning Christians or the church) being the Bride of Christ. If I take that passage seriously, I'm convinced that it's important not to dishonor or demean His Bride. It seems like people haven't thought about how Jesus feels about anyone verbally abusing or disparaging His Bride.

Psalm 31:19–20 says,

How great is Your goodness, which You have stored up for those who reverently fear You. In the secret place of Your presence You hide them from the plots and conspiracies of man; You keep them from the strife of tongues. (AMP)

When I read this, my heart leapt because I have actually experienced this stuff in real life! God has goodness stored up for us. As we fear the Lord, He blesses us, but what does that mean?

The fear of the Lord, for me, has to do with respect and reverence for individual people, people in the Body of Christ, and especially the leaders. Scripture says that the church is the Bride of Christ, and is actually His treasured possession (see Deut 7:6). My respect for individuals is motivated not by their sterling character or performance, but in my desire to honor what God is doing in their lives. He is committed to see Christ formed in each one, so I'm partnering with Him to see His will come to pass.

This is true on an even more heightened level when it comes to criticizing local churches and their leaders. I call it *throwing rocks.* I really can't see how God can bless me if I throw rocks or tear down the work of the Kingdom in someone else's church.

The secret is found in the words, "those who take refuge in you." That beautiful phrase involves believing, trusting, and choosing to allow God to advocate for us, vindicate us, and defend us. We ask Him to cover us with His presence; He comes and covers us, hides us and shelters us from plots and strife. This is a great truth: He hides us from the plots and strife of other people. This is a divine protection over our hearts and minds.

The Holy Spirit teaches us how to not participate in mudslinging and backbiting. I read recently on Pinterest, "You don't have to attend every argument you're invited to." I'll admit it. It took me a while to learn that it isn't in my best interest to know and discuss the imperfections of other people. It robs my peace to wrap my brain around issues over which I have no control.

In some cases, it is possible that you find yourself unable to give of yourself in good faith to a local assembly because the leader or the corporate vision has changed. That is the point where you say, "Thanks for the ride. This is my stop." It's way better to sweetly bless a congregation and then to go find a new church home, rather than to stay and stir up dissension and strife. I'm a peacemaker. "Blessed are the peacemakers, for they shall be called sons of God" (Matt 5:9).

I choose to exchange my turmoil for His peace. Then, I am in a position to experience His abundant goodness in the form of His wondrous steadfast love, protection, and peace. The bottom line for me is this: I don't throw rocks at other people's ministries because I don't think it honors God, and He already knows His church has flaws.

The other reason I don't criticize church leaders is because I believe that the Chief Shepherd is always faithful to the sheep. Ezekiel 34:15 (ESV) says, "I myself will be the shepherd of my sheep, and I myself will make them lie down, declares the Lord God." The chapter goes into detail about how much God cares for us, His sheep, and that never changes. He is committed to caring for me. Ultimately, His care is where I put my trust, not in people, and He never fails.

"Let Her Eat"

Yesterday, I took my darling mother to a neurologist to rule out the possibility of dementia. She's eighty-five, and she's still really adorable. She has been having trouble with her short-term memory and especially word recall. I must admit that her ability to summon a particular word was quite bad. I'd never seen her like this, but my sister had.

The doctor's office wasn't in a traditional medical suite or neurology practice, but rather in a medium-sized hospital of its own, a whole neurology facility—Dent Tower. Doctor Dent must be some visionary guy. "Brains R Us," I'm thinking.

The reception area was a little shabby, kind of like a Manhattan hotel that had seen a whole lot of school trips. The clerical staff was friendly; they had us fill out multiple pages of information which I did for my mom. When I was finished, my mom made me go back and fix my spelling errors. "You spelled the medicine wrong. Think it matters?"

I fixed it.

The intake person was a sweet-faced girl with no make-up on. She could have been nineteen or thirty. I couldn't tell. She gave my mom a little battery of questions to check on her mental abilities, stuff like the date, her address, "What happened on September 11th?" She scored 26 out of 30. Not bad.

The doctor came in and was a middle-aged guy who had a face full of care and optimism at the same time. He had a heavy accent, and when I asked him about his country of origin, he said he was Hungarian. He asked us about my mother's history with the trouble, and I recounted the tough season she had been having with urinary tract infections (UTIs). He said that the disorientation from a UTI can last up to four weeks. I was relieved because she had had four of them since May. She had four weeks between them, so I was asking God to heal her and to give her a clear mind, not that she's ever had a great short-term memory. She at least needed her words back.

The doctor said that the first order of business was to get her to a urologist to find out why she was repeatedly getting these infections. Good idea!

After that, we went to Wegmans to eat off their marvelous buffet, which always makes me feel as though I've been invited to a really great wedding. (So glad I don't have to bring a gift.)

I got a salad and a piece of fish. I looked at my mom's plate and hers was filled with deep-fried spicy chicken wings and three strawberries. I said, "Mom, don't you want a green vegetable with that?"

She said, "No, I'm sick of vegetables."

The checkout person overheard me, and she said, "How old is she?"

"Eighty-five," I answered.

"Life is short. Let her eat the damned chicken wings."

Sometimes, life is too short to go with my idealized policies about low fat and low carbs. Sometimes, you have to see the larger picture which involves celebrations of eighty-five-year-olds who are still funny and feisty like my mom, and some moments are better enjoyed with chicken wings and ice cream.

Hungry for More

L AST WEEK MY MOTHER'S BROTHER, Gene, passed away. He had just celebrated his eighty-sixth birthday. He had eight kids. His funeral made me revisit this strange truth that people can grow up in the same family and yet be so different in their temperament, coping, and thinking styles.

The people who spoke at the funeral generally spoke of what a fun guy my uncle was, how he liked to have parties, and that he was a hard worker. My mom, on the other hand, is a pensive, sensitive, abstract thinker. Her mother was born in Scotland, and her dad was born in France. Even though her mother spoke English, culturally they were new to this country, and I don't think that they knew all the dance steps of city living or public schools in the U.S.

Her parents worked in restaurants and bars. They repaired roofs and pretty much did whatever they could to make ends meet. I think her brother and sisters grew up early, and all married in their teens except my mom.

Mom, for some reason, has the distinct quality of always wondering if there's more. She left home at nineteen and toured the country, did clerical work along the way, but the common theme was the nagging curiosity that there was more meaning to this life than what she had known so far. That's why, even though she eventually married and had four of her own kids, her thirst for satisfaction and significance eventually led her to a tiny little white,pentecostal church in a blue-collar suburb of Buffalo. "This church has a Dixie-land jazz band," was what she was told. "You have to hear it!" Her sister prodded her.

I get the feeling that, at forty years old, the message of God's grace and redeeming power gave my mom that Eureka moment of finally finding the thing she had been searching for.

She still has that quality of wanting more. It translates into desiring deeper experiences with God in worship and in prayer, chasing revival, and an inexhaustible thirst for knowing Him.

G.K. Beale says that people will always have longings that can only be satisfied in God's presence, because in the beginning we were created for the garden of Eden, where we had uninterrupted fellowship with a loving God. We hunger for the satisfaction and significance that came from being in perfect communication with the Father. It mystifies me why some people sense their need and others don't. My prayer is that a hunger would bubble up in all my family and my relatives would become spiritually thirsty for more, and that includes me, by the way.

Family Recipe

I LOOK AT THE CHILDREN OF my peers who are continuing in their faith that started way back in VBS. Their faith started smack dab in the middle of graham crackers and apple juice, back before snacks were cool stuff like Doritos. (If you were lucky, the animal crackers were fresh.) These kids responded to the question, "Do you want Jesus to come live in your heart and take away your sins?"

They said, "Yes," before they were even able to read those same words, while sitting cross-legged on carpeting that smelled a little moldy. They heard Bible stories that told them to trust and pray like Daniel and Esther. We told them to be brave like David and the three Hebrews in Babylon, and to be honest like Joseph in Egypt. In large measure, that's what they're doing.

These young people remind me of the passage in Deuteronomy 6, where it says the children of Israel were led into the Promised Land to inherit "great cities that they did not build, cisterns and wells that [they] did not dig and vineyards and groves that [they] did not plant."

The young adults I know are not only physically beautiful, but also trained in the way of godliness that distilled down from the hard lessons learned by their parents. They never experienced the pain of parents not approving of their faith. They never had family who rejected and condemned their faith, who said it was a crutch for the weak, while demonstrating destructive patterns of substance abuse or weird, extreme codependences. In my own case, my mother wasn't all that mature in her faith, but at least she endorsed me.

The vineyard they inherit is the beginning of a life of prayer and knowing what it's like to have the Holy Spirit visit them in their quiet time with His new wine. Biblical principles, like tithing, don't sound like a foreign language. Missionary service and giving is not alien; it's normal. All of this beautiful framework is in place because someone had the guts and the grace to pioneer a new lineage of faith.

The challenge for anyone who grew up in a faith-filled environment is to realize that even though you inherited something—a beautiful and precious like faith—it still needs to be tended to and guarded on a very personal level. Deuteronomy says that this inheritance must be kept by diligently remembering the slavery from which your parents were delivered. Maybe for some it was many generations ago.

Tend the vineyards that were entrusted to you by God Himself. Identify the areas where your parents taught you legalistic, unscriptural rules. Forgive them. Root out what threatens or destroys. And then, enjoy it! Use the vast, expansive inheritance to innovative new adventures that glorify the King and in turn produce something glorious!

Acknowledgments

I AM DEEPLY INDEBTED TO MY friend and editor, Edie Mourey at Furrow Press, who spent countless hours with me on the phone and in person helping me take my 'drawer full of beads' and making it into a 'necklace.' You helped me format this manuscript; your guidance and patience have been a gift to me.

I am so grateful for my pastors, Pierre and Marlize duPlessis and my Father's House family in Rochester, NY. Thank you for being a gentle 'on ramp' for people to enter the Kingdom of God.

Thank you for understanding the lost, and serving them so well.

A giant shout of gratitude goes out to my dearest sister-friend, Sue Jenks. You've believed in me and relentlessly cheered me on with wisdom and generosity. Your selfless support and shared love for Mexican food have made this book possible. I'm so thankful to have you in my life.

To my mom, Violet, thank you for modeling what it looks like to relentlessly pursue more intimacy with the Holy Spirit and more love for the Lord Jesus. Your passion for the lost and local church inspires me. You are a pioneer who is leaving a legacy of faith and I'm eternally grateful.

To my daughters, Lily and Grace, my son, David, and my daughter-in-law, Katie, you have been a constant source of joy, more than I could ever have imagined. You have brought meaning and order to my life and without you I wouldn't have a reason to say anything.

And to Karl, the man of my dreams, who has ushered the Kingdom of God into my life with his redemptive brand of unconditional love. Your servant leadership and your protective care are not only a gift to our family, but to everyone you know. Thank you for facilitating my dreams. You are my flag pole; I am your flag. I love you so much.

About The Author

BONNY'S PASSION IS FOR NURTURING, empowering and inspiring men and women to love deeply, act bravely and live brilliantly. She believes that God transforms us through prayer, his Word, and his people, and that each of us is a living example of his redeeming love. She believes that God can truly heal the world through us.

She graduated from Elim Bible Institute and College and holds a B.S.Ed from Roberts Wesleyan College. She holds a Masters in Education from Nazareth College of Rochester, NY.

Bonny is ordained through Elim Fellowship.

She and her husband, Karl, attend The Father's House in Rochester, where she is part of the teaching team. Together they run a vibrant weekly young adult ministry.

She and Karl, love being parents to Lily, Grace, David and his beautiful wife, Katie!

52736428R00119

Made in the USA
Lexington, KY
19 September 2019